12

EASY STEPS TO

Successful

Research Papers

Second Edition

12 EASY STEPS TO
Successful
Research Papers

Nell W. Meriwether

 **Glencoe**

New York, New York   Columbus, Ohio   Chicago, Illinois   Peoria, Illinois   Woodland Hills, California

Cover design: Carolyn Deacy, Carolyn Deacy Design
Cover illustrations: Mary Rich
Interior illustrations: Ophelia M. Chambliss

The McGraw·Hill Companies

Send all Inquiries to:
Glencoe/McGraw-Hill
8787 Orion Place
Columbus, OH 43240

ISBN :   0-658-00117-5
Printed in the United States of America
3 4 5 6 7 8 9 10 <u>113</u>   08 07 06 05 04

Meriwether, Nell.
    12 easy steps to successful research papers / Nell W. Meriwether.— 2nd ed.
        p. cm. — (12 easy steps to—)
    Includes index.
    ISBN 0-658-00117-5
    1. Report writing—Handbooks, manuals, etc. 2. Research—Handbooks, manuals, etc. I. Title: Twelve easy steps to successful research papers. II. Title. III. Series.

LB1047.3 .M47 2000
371.3'028'1—dc21

                                                                    00-42387

Contents

STEP 5

STEP 6

STEP 7

STEP 8

STEP 9

STEP 10

STEP 11

STEP 12

PREFACE

After more than twenty-five years of teaching students how to write a research paper, I realized that what I really needed to do was to gather all of the information I had taught into a book that could be used by students for many years to come. The result is *12 Easy Steps to Successful Research Papers*, a compilation of ideas I have developed over the years. This book is unique in that the directions for writing a research paper are simple enough for even the neophyte writer to understand. By following the step-by-step process explored within, anyone can write a successful research paper.

While it maintains the twelve easy steps and straightforward approach of the first edition, this second edition has been revised and updated in several ways. First and foremost, it includes a gathering of new information having to do with computer research and the World Wide Web, reflecting the way research is really done today. The section on evaluating sources has been expanded to recognize the fact that in this era of information, more care needs to be taken to determine what are credible sources. And, in addition to the examples that are provided at each step throughout the book, there are three complete research papers in the appendices. The first research paper on Tourette Syndrome in Appendix A is developed step-by-step in the text.

As anyone knows, writing a book takes much time and effort. I, therefore, wish to express my appreciation to my husband, Carl L. Meriwether, for his support and encouragement, and to Cathy Seal, Phyllis Heroy, Pat Bordelon, and especially Mike MacDonald for helping me with the latest in computer research.

Nell W. Meriwether

INTRODUCTION

If you have never written a research paper before, you may think you are facing an overwhelming task. Your instructor may have told you the number of pages you must write, the number of sources you must consult, and the number of note cards you must compile—and the job seems impossible. You may not have written anything of this magnitude before.

But writing a research paper can be a straightforward task. The twelve steps in this text will explain the process to you clearly and concisely. You will find as you do your research that other people have thought along similar lines, and you will be able to use their ideas to support yours. And, after you have learned these steps, you may even find writing a research paper to be an enjoyable challenge. After all, it will probably be the first of many research papers you will write either in school or on the job. Thus, what you learn now will be invaluable to you later.

So, welcome to the world of research—a world you will find interesting as well as informative; a world that will become yours by mastering a few simple steps.

The steps you will follow are given below. They are logical and sequential—that is, you should follow them in order. If you follow these steps, you will see how well they fit together, and you should have little difficulty in writing your paper.

1. Choose a subject.
2. Narrow the subject into a manageable topic.
3. Research your material.
4. Get information for your bibliography.
5. Take notes on note cards.
6. Form a thesis.
7. Make an outline.
8. Add the references to your paper.
9. Write the first draft.
10. Compile the Works Cited page.
11. Revise your paper.
12. Write the final copy.

S T E P

1

Choosing a Subject

The first step in writing a research paper is to decide on a subject. Your instructor may give you a specific subject, especially if the paper is on a literary topic. On the other hand, you may be allowed to choose your own subject. If so, you should choose a subject in which you have some interest. You may not know much about the subject at the moment, but that is what research is all about—discovering and learning.

If you have not been given an assigned subject, there are several methods to help you select a subject that appeals to you, which can be used for either a literary or a nonliterary subject. Once you decide on which type—literary or nonliterary—you can then determine which technique will work best for you. Since you are experimenting at this point, and will be working with this subject for several weeks, you may want to try more than one of the methods given for finding a subject.

FINDING A SUBJECT

The general techniques for finding a subject include brainstorming, asking questions, clustering, freewriting or looping, outlining, and scanning books and videos. Additional ideas are discussed under FINDING A NONLITER-ARY SUBJECT and FINDING A LITERARY SUBJECT. Each of these techniques is discussed here with suggestions about how to use them to select a topic for your research.

FINDING A NONLITERARY SUBJECT

If you have not been assigned a topic, the following are several methods for finding a topic that appeals to you.

Brainstorming

Think of a subject that you are already interested in and would like to know more about. It could be one of your current hobbies or one that you are curious about, a place you have read about or have seen in a documentary, or even a culture you find fascinating because of its dress, religion, customs, or foods.

You can brainstorm on your own, or you may want to pool your ideas with other students. Brainstorming with others often brings out many ideas that will help you choose a subject. For example, some of the subjects that members of one class chose were bungee jumping, Himalayan Indian culture and religion, archaeological digs in Israel, AIDS research, and South Pole experiments.

One student, Mike, perked up when he learned that the research paper could be about something of interest to him. He had earned the badge of Eagle Scout and loved scouting. He had been hiking at Philmont, New Mexico, one summer and had gone on numerous camping trips. Because of his interest in scouting, he felt that would be a good research topic. Another student, Janice, was interested in stock-car racing. She wanted to find out why there are so few female drivers, so she chose to research the subject.

Because of their previous interests in these subjects, Mike and Janice were ready to start immediately. Other students became just as excited when they began talking about what could be a subject for their research, and their final papers showed their enthusiasm.

Asking Questions

Another useful method for discovering what to write about is to ask friends or family members what they find unusual or interesting. Perhaps someone you know is a member of an unusual group or has a fascinating occupation, such as working as a foreign correspondent, a jockey, or a stuntwoman. All of these people started out as ordinary individuals who developed a fascination for unusual occupations. As you talk to them, you probably will want to discover more about their interests. Then you would research these particular occupations.

Clustering

Clustering is a prewriting technique that helps you to associate ideas so that you can discover relationships you perhaps hadn't realized worked well together. Basically, it works like this: Put the broad subject you think might have potential at the top of the page. Then write down all of the ideas that come to your mind that could possibly be associated with the subject. Next, circle those that seem to fit together, drawing lines connecting them. Keep associating and connecting as long as you can. After all, the more ideas you have, the better, for then you will discover more ideas for research.

Let me give you an example. One student, Bob Atwater, was interested in wild turkey hunting. He often visited his grandfather who lived in the country. Bob wanted to find out more about the sport, so he put at the top of the page the words "Wild Turkey Hunting." Then he quickly jotted down the following words and phrases:

Grandpa	turkey rifles	when to shoot or not shoot
bait or no bait	type of shot used	turkey calling
proper clothing	turkey blinds	rules for shooting
which turkeys not to shoot	recipes for turkey	season and time of year
when turkey shooting became a sport		
Uncle Ben's story of the one that got away		

Of course, Bob was not limited to these ideas, but as he looked at them, he circled those that seemed to fit together and drew lines connecting them. To illustrate, he connected *turkey rifles* to *type of shot used*. *Rules for shooting* was connected to *when to shoot*. Then he joined *season* and *time of year* with *proper clothing*. He drew a line to *Grandpa* and *turkey calling* since Grandpa made turkey callers. As he completed his clustering, he realized that some ideas might not fit into his paper, and he added other ideas that came to mind. But clustering helped Bob realize he already knew quite a bit to base his research on. Now he was ready to start delving into those aspects of turkey hunting with which he wasn't as familiar.

Freewriting and/or Looping

Freewriting is what its name implies—writing freely about a subject in order to determine if you have anything to say about it. This can be done in class as the instructor times you in intervals, or it can be done on your own. Freewriting is a technique that is very similar to a prewriting technique called looping. The difference is that with looping you write a sentence at the end of each loop called a center of gravity sentence. That sentence sums up what has been said in the loop and gives you a starting point for the next loop. That is why the activity is called looping. One loop flows into the other loop through the center of gravity sentence.

The rules for freewriting and looping are very simple. Anything goes! Punctuation is not important nor are complete sentences or the order of your thoughts. What is important is to get your ideas down on paper.

Often the instructor will time the class for three to five periods, or loops, with each period lasting from five to ten minutes. After your first timed writing, you should be able to discover if you have anything to say about the subject. If not, you can change the subject to one with which you are more familiar. The point is that the more you write, the more material you will have as ideas for your research. Then you can choose what is important, what is not needed, and what needs to be enlarged upon in your work. A note of caution, though, concerning this prewriting exercise: it is not the same as the first draft of your paper. The first draft of your paper will be much longer and more focused.

Outlining

Outlining is another technique that is often used. It consists of putting the thoughts you have about the subject in a rough outline form. With this method, you already have some idea of what you want to focus upon for your research. What you will do with it depends upon the organization of your thoughts, which necessarily will expand as you research your topic.

Carolyn used an example of this approach in her paper. She wanted to research the possibilities of having a book of her poems published. She had already created many of them. She knew there were certain things she had to do, but she wasn't sure she knew how to go about the process. She jotted down the following ideas and then arranged them so that they formed an outline she could work with.

1. Getting the poems in a good working format
2. Choosing which poems to use
   a. Deciding whether to group poems into subjects
   b. Determining whether to group poems according to kinds of poems
3. Talking with poets who have had poems published
4. Reading poetry that is similar
5. Buying books that deal with poetry publications
6. Learning how to write query letters and submit ideas to publishers
7. Checking in the library for ideas about getting published
8. Determining if poetry has reader appeal
9. Deciding on the format of the book
10. Considering self publication (money involved)

From this list, Carolyn outlined her paper, throwing out those ideas she deemed unnecessary and adding others. Notice that she did not include examples of her poetry that she could use to emphasize a point in her research, nor did she include a time frame for book proposals to be returned by editors. These she may decide to use later, but at least she has a good working idea of what she will include.

Scanning Books and Videos

If you still draw a blank on what to write, go to the library and look in the indexes in an area that interests you. For example, if you are interested in a particular period of history, look in the index of books dealing with history. Subjects such as the Great Depression, the Roaring Twenties, the Harlem Renaissance, or the Reconstruction of the South will stand out. As you scan these topics and others, you will probably be able to find a topic that interests you.

Another place to look for a subject is a bookstore or even a video rental store, which can be a springboard for research in your school or local library. Just looking at the titles of books and videos and their placement in the stores will often give you a subject to research. For example, Jane was uncertain about a subject. She went to the video store and found one section devoted to children's cartoons. As she looked at the titles, she became interested in what the cartoons were teaching children. Many of them seemed to contain violence. Her research led her to various groups that were advocating censorship of children's programs and cartoons. Jane's investigation proved not only to be the subject of her research, but it also became a project she continued to work on after she turned in her research paper.

Choosing a Topic of Personal Interest

From the six prewriting techniques already given, you probably have a pretty good idea which one will help you most in choosing a subject. However, if you are still having problems determining what to write about, you may want to think of a topic of a more personal nature.

The following suggestions may help you recall something you have always wanted to know more about. You may want to research a debilitating illness of a friend, or you may have a family member who died at an early age with an unusual disease and are concerned for your own well being. You may choose to find out about a landmark in your community that was destroyed, or why an area you have lived in seems to be tornado prone. All you have to do is to open your mind, and many subjects will emerge that would be good research material.

Look at the three prewriting techniques here and see how exciting it would be to research using one of them.

Personal Inventory

Personal inventory simply means choosing a subject you are already interested in and familiar with. You are actually taking an inventory of what is in your storehouse of knowledge, just as a store takes an inventory of what is inside.

For example, as you inventory yourself, you become aware of a number of things that are of interest to you. These may be contemporary art and artists, various styles of music, or horse racing and the Kentucky Derby. Perhaps your interests lie in politics and the role of women or minorities in political office. The point is that you have a far greater range of interests than you may have originally thought. All that you need to do is hone in on one of these interests and compile a list of ideas to develop. From these ideas you can begin researching your paper.

Researching Your Family

Why not research your own family? Instead of the familiar family tree of genealogical research, talk to someone in your extended family whom you find interesting. Perhaps he or she did something unusual or lived in an exotic place. Maybe he or she lived during World War II or helped in the Civil Rights movement or came as an immigrant from another country during a time of great duress. Develop your research by enlarging on this particular person and what made him or her interesting.

As you work on this idea, enlarge your focus to include the time period in which the person lived and the problems encountered. You would want to consider the person's unusual activities and effects on your family and perhaps society. Your paper, then, would not be simply a reporting of your family but would require research of a more objective nature.

Lan, another student, came to America during the Vietnam conflict. On the way over, her father was taken off the boat on which she and the rest of her family were crowded. She never saw him again. Her research project softened some of her bitter memories as she searched her family tree and found men and women who were brave and who dared to stand up for their beliefs. Lan's paper, though personal, was written objectively. She wrote in such a way that others would want to hear of the bravery and courage of people fleeing a country to find freedom to live without the hardships of war.

Researching a Point of Interest

You may have wanted to know more about a debilitating illness a family member or friend had, and you never had the time to really research the subject. For example, one student, Gene, was diagnosed with Chronic Fatigue Syndrome in his senior year of high school. He had never even heard of the disease before. All he knew was that he had no energy and that some days he was hardly able to drag himself from the bed. He missed school often. As a result of the diagnosis, he decided his research paper would be about

Chronic Fatigue Syndrome. He had a "ready-made" subject. You may not have had that kind of experience, but you may know of something else in the medical field that intrigues you. Perhaps you want to know more about a rare disease that caused the death of a family member at a young age.

Another idea for determining your subject is to think of your own community. Your interest may be piqued about an old home or building in your area that has historical value and is about to be razed. You feel strongly that it should be preserved because of its history. Your research could take you in the direction of having it restored and kept in the National Registry of Historical Places. This would depend, of course, on your making a creditable case for the local authorities so that they also could see the value in having the building restored. Not only would you find this subject interesting, but it may also benefit the community.

A final suggestion for researching a point of interest is to consider where you live. Many parts of the country are prone to tornadoes or floods or droughts. Because you live in that particular area, research into the logistics of weather and weather patterns and what can be done to make the area more habitable might be of real interest. Ideas for your research would be the viability of better building codes, better warning systems, and even more adequate government controls. Because of your living in the area, this topic would be of personal interest and could prove valuable to others.

Research papers that deal with topics such as those given lend themselves to personal experiences that include the use of personal pronouns. However, the paper itself should still be written objectively, making it more sophisticated and of more interest to others.

It is true that some writers, such as William Zinsser in *On Writing Well*, suggest that the first person be used in particular kinds of writing. Still, for most research papers, writing from the third-person or the objective point of view is better style. Using third-person pronouns—*he, his, him, she, hers, her, they, their,* and *them*—is much better than using the first-person pronouns—*I, me, mine, we, us, our,* and *ours*. Third-person pronouns change the total outlook of your paper. It becomes more objective and is therefore of more interest to more readers. After all, the research paper is your thinking except for those parts that are documented, thus making the first person unnecessary.

Another point to consider when choosing a nonliterary subject, whether it is of a personal nature or simply a topic of interest, is to be careful not to narrow your thinking too much. You need enough resources available on the subject for you to do thorough research, especially if you are writing the kind of paper in which you present an argument and then defend your position. A research paper on a historical site to be preserved might be a case in point. In fact, the more resources you have, the better your defense.

From these techniques having to do with the nonliterary paper, you should be able to determine which prewriting technique best suits the assignment. You must keep in mind, however, that the subject you choose must not be too technical or your audience will be unable to understand your research. At the same time, it should have some interest for your audience.

FINDING A LITERARY SUBJECT

Suppose you have been given a literary subject, and you need to narrow it down to a topic for your paper. You could focus your thoughts in more than one direction, two of which are given here.

Literary Genre

The literary genre approach means that you will be using standard literary criticism to critique a particular genre, such as fiction, biography, drama, poetry, short stories, nonfiction, essays, or others. Because these areas are broad, you still need to subdivide your thinking. For example, if you were researching fiction, you would subdivide the term *fiction* into historical fiction or historical romance, escape fiction, science fiction, mystery, or other types of fiction.

In order to determine if you have enough knowledge to adequately critique one of these genres, you could use one of the prewriting techniques already discussed. Brainstorming, asking questions, and clustering lend themselves well to a literary topic. A thorough knowledge of the subject is paramount to writing an acceptable paper, and using many resources is a must.

Literary Terms

Many literary terms lend themselves well to research. Examples include elegy, fable, myth, parable, satire, and figurative language. Each of these terms can be a subject of its own with adequate examples throughout literature, but we will use the term *satire* to give you an idea of how other terms may be developed.

As you begin to think about satire, you may remember short stories, novels, poems, or essays that you have read that are satirical. For example, in his poem, "To a Louse," Robert Burns satirizes a fashionable young lady with a louse on her bonnet. Samuel Johnson's "Letter to Lord Chesterfield" is a scathing attack on the man who was his supposed patron while Johnson was writing his dictionary. The American humorist James Thurber satirizes people through his caricatures of people behaving like animals and animals behaving like people in day-to-day predicaments. C. S. Lewis also uses satire in his book *Screwtape Letters* in which he makes fun of the way the devil tempts people.

In addition to looking at various works that use satire, you may also consider the various forms of satire, such as Juvenalian and Horatian. You may want to delve into the origin of satire or the use of satire in television and other forms of modern media. The *I Love Lucy* comedy series, which pokes fun at the antics of the American housewife, or *Saturday Night Live* sketches, which use anything and anybody as subject matter, may help you to define your topic. Another option would be to research a modern comic-strip artist, such as Garry Trudeau, creator of "Doonesbury," whose views of social and political issues are shown in his comic strip. You could research the great eighteenth century satirist Jonathan Swift, who wrote "A Modest Proposal," in which he advocates selling babies for food in order to lower the population of Ireland and help alleviate poverty in the country. You could choose John Gardner, a modern humorist who writes using dark or black humor, as he describes the senselessness and meanness of human life in his story of *Grendel*, a retelling of the Old English epic *Beowulf*.

The point is that as you think about a particular genre of literature or about a particular literary term or another idea that has surfaced, your problem becomes one of figuring out what to include. You will find there is an abundance of material rather than not enough material to research. You will begin to determine, through following the guidelines in the next step, which material is of value and which needs to be discarded. In this way, you will learn how to evaluate your material so that you can reduce your subject into a manageable topic.

EXERCISE 1 Library Research

1. Look in an encyclopedia—print or electronic—for a subject that interests you.

2. After you have found the subject, determine the time period—if your subject is biographical—in order to be able to find other resources.

3. Next, search the card catalog—print or electronic—and write down or print out the call numbers of books on the subject.

4. Research the reference section of the library and write down at least five sources that you could use in your search for a subject. These could include print media, such as *The Reader's Guide to Periodical Literature* or the electronic *Reader's Guide*. In addition, you might also choose an Internet Search Engine or Directory Service Provider such as Copernic or Webcompass or WebSeeker or others for possible sources.

5. From these sources, choose one strong subject that you think would be interesting to research. Prepare to discuss your choice in class.

EXERCISE 2 Outside Research

1. Go to either a bookstore or a video rental store and write down at least six classifications of books or videos. Examples are classical, suspense movies, comedies, drama, and musicals.

2. Choose one that most interests you from this list.

3. From the classification, further narrow the category. For example, if you choose suspense movies, you might narrow the category to Hitchcock suspense movies or remakes of classic suspense films.

4. Determine a subject you think would be interesting to research.

5. At the library, find at least five resources for your selection, using the card catalog and the reference section of the library as well as electronic online services.

2

Narrowing the Subject into a Manageable Topic

By now you have a broad idea of your subject. The next step is to narrow it to a manageable size because it is impossible to write a research paper on all aspects of any subject. Narrowing the subject helps you focus your research. It gives you direction and keeps you from taking notes on material that does not pertain to your paper. By following the process here, you will find that narrowing your subject is easier than you first thought.

NARROWING YOUR SUBJECT INTO A TOPIC

One of the best ways to narrow your subject to a workable topic is to use research questions. You can develop these through brainstorming or by using the lead questions that are used in journalism: the five *W*s and the *H*—*who, what, when, where, why,* and *how*.

If you were researching a general subject such as the Persian Gulf War, your questions might look like the following:

1. *What* do you know about this subject already?
   What were the causes of the Persian Gulf War?
   What caused the conflict to escalate to that point?
   What happened as a result of the war?
   What diseases were contracted during the war?
   What countries were involved?
2. *Who* was involved?
   Who were the leaders of the nations involved?
3. *Where* did the Persian Gulf War happen? In which country?
   Where were American forces stationed?
4. *When* did it happen?
   When were the years of the war?
5. *Why* is the information important?
   Why was the Persian Gulf War necessary?
6. *How* did it begin?
   How many were killed or injured in the war?

These questions do not tell you a great deal by themselves, but they start you on the investigative process. They help you determine the direction to go, and they give you questions to consider as you begin your research. You may choose to follow the course of the war from beginning to end, or you may want to research the causes of the war. You may even want to research what happened as a result of the war. This could lead you in the direction of whether the goals of the war were met or what the effects of the war were on the nations involved. You may research the war's effect on different groups of people, such as the soldiers or civilians in the country. By using this investigative process, you will develop an idea of what to focus on in your paper. In other words, you are now ready to narrow the general subject of the Persian Gulf War to a more specific topic.

To apply these questions to a literary subject, you use the same process. Suppose you have been given the general subject of John Steinbeck's novel, *The Grapes of Wrath*. Naturally, the first thing to do is to read the book, but simply reading the book will not be enough for you to decide on the direction for your paper. The book will be the focal point from which to work, but it in itself cannot be your entire research paper. You will want to research other important ideas you discovered while reading. Investigative questions, such as the following, can be used:

1. *What* is this book's lesson for mankind?
   What different circumstances distinguish the book's characters from other people who have left their homes and become migrants?
   What caused the government to change its thinking about conservation?
2. *When* was the Dust Bowl that caused such a migration of people?
3. *Where* did the events take place?
   Where did the Okies and the Arkies and others come face-to-face with people who feared them because of their sheer poverty and numbers?
4. *Who* was involved?
   Who should bear the responsibility for these conditions?
5. *Why* were these events so important for these conditions?
   Why did it take such dire circumstances before drastic measures were taken by the government?
6. *How* did it happen?
   How did people survive with absolutely nothing?
   How did exposing the living conditions of the migrants affect laws designed to care for the land as well as for the migrants?

By using questions such as these, you can see that there is much more to your subject than one book can provide. A host of topics has emerged from reading a single book. Perhaps one topic would be the effect on legislation of Steinbeck's exposure of migrant conditions. Another might be researching the Dust Bowl and its causes and effects, which resulted in the migration of thousands of people to California. You might even consider other books of social protest that have helped change society. For example, Upton Sinclair exposed conditions in the meat-packing industry in *The Jungle*, which helped bring about pure food and drug laws. Whatever aspect you choose, your paper will be more thorough because you have investigated many topics that reading the book has opened to you.

Your instructor may assign you a particular type of paper to write, or he or she may give you the freedom to choose the type you prefer. Whichever is the case, keep in mind that knowing the type of paper will help you in gathering material. For example, with an informative paper that deals mostly with facts, you will be researching for information on your topic. But with a persuasive paper, you will want to get information for both sides of your argument—both pros and cons—in order to convince your reader of your ideas. Knowing the type of paper also will help you determine whether you will write a comparison/contrast paper, a cause and effect paper, a literary analysis, or some other form of writing.

In narrowing your search for the topic, you will find that you can use investigative questions for almost any subject. Thinking critically about your subject and asking these questions helps open your mind to ideas you may have never considered.

To help you understand the process of actually writing the research paper, this book will take a subject, narrow it to a topic, and then go through each step of writing the paper. As indicated in Step 1, a good way to decide on a research subject is to look around you for points of interest. One of those indicated was an illness that was debilitating to someone you knew or that you simply wanted more information on. With the many problems having to do with children's health today, the general subject of health was chosen as the broad topic for the research paper for this book. You can see from the following diagram that the field of health problems for children is very encompassing. Even though the list is not conclusive, all of the entries show possibilities for research. The decision, then, is which problem would be more interesting than others to research or even which problem might generate more interest to other people. Look at the way the topics seemingly relate to each other, which may or may not help in determining the final subject to be researched.

Childhood Health Problems

Measles	Rheumatoid Arthritis
Mumps	Heart Problems
Hyperactivity	Stuttering/Speech Problems
Hearing Problems	Vision Problems
Hypertension	Attention Deficit Disorder
Asthma	Tourette Syndrome
Chronic Fatigue Syndrome	

After looking at each of the problems given and how they seemingly relate to each other, the two that seem most interesting are Chronic Fatigue Syndrome and Tourette Syndrome, perhaps because these problems have surfaced more in recent years. They also affect many areas of a child's life. It is easy to see, too, that researching either of these topics could be informative or argumentative. The paper could be informative, giving information about the disease itself and its effect on children. Or the paper could be persuasive, arguing that more research needs to be done to determine the causes of the disease and possible cures.

As one of the prewriting techniques suggested, one way to determine how to choose a topic is asking others about what they know of the two illnesses. One student, Ellen, had a friend whose son had Tourette Syndrome, a disease that she and her friend wanted to know more about. Because of her interest and because there is still so much to be known, the student decided to write about Tourette Syndrome, a problem with no known cure. We will follow her progress as she develops her paper and then will give her completed research paper in Appendix A.

The student asked the following investigative questions:

1. <u>What</u> is Tourette Syndrome?

   <u>What</u> does it involve?

   <u>What</u> research has been done about Tourette?

2. <u>Who</u> usually has Tourette?

3. <u>Where</u> does it affect the person?

4. <u>When</u> does it usually start?

5. <u>Why</u> is knowing about Tourette important?

   <u>Why</u> hasn't a cure been found?

6. <u>How</u> is Tourette recognized?

   <u>How</u> is Tourette treated?

   <u>How</u> do the other family members learn to cope?

Other questions also surfaced: Are there Tourette Syndrome support groups? Are there many people affected with Tourette? Can a person live a normal life with Tourette? Does having Tourette Syndrome affect one's longevity? Is the person inhibited intellectually? Can he or she participate in sports? Is it possible the person's offspring will have Tourette?

You can see a research paper emerging with these questions, so in narrowing the general subject of Childhood Health Problems to Tourette Sydrome, the student's first consideration was what is already known about the subject in a general way. The problem was in which direction to go; should she research from a purely scientific study or from a more informal, human interest point of view? Ellen's first consideration was to decide on the audience for the paper, because this would affect the tone and style of her paper. She went to the next step in the investigative process—knowing where to begin—in order to find the answers to her questions.

EXPLORING SOURCES TO HELP NARROW YOUR SUBJECT

Because of modern technology, the first place you will probably begin your search will be the electronic media. The card catalog, which is electronic in most libraries now, is still a good place to begin because it contains information about all of the books in the library. As with the traditional card catalog, you can search your topic by title, author, and subject matter. With the electronic card catalog, you are also able to scan for topics within the books themselves. And an added feature is that you can print out a list of available material so that you do not have to write everything down.

The reference section in the library is also a good place to help you determine if you will have enough material for your research. It includes reference books, periodical indexes, and electronic sources and databases. Electronic online full-text services are available for your use through these databases. As you research a subject, such as the Persian Gulf War, migrants, the Dust Bowl, satire, or Tourette Syndrome, you can read what other people have already researched on your subject.

Electronic sources, such as Disclit *American Authors* CD-ROM or *Magazine Article Summaries* CD-ROM, as well as non-CD online sources, are also useful in determining research topics. In addition, *The Electronic Encyclopedia* and many other reference sets are on CD-ROM. These sources bring up needed information quickly and efficiently, and the research can be printed in a matter of minutes.

As will be discussed in Step 3, your problem with the World Wide Web will be in narrowing your focus to one subject since there is so much material available. Finding enough material will usually not be the problem; the problem will be in which direction to go to limit your thinking and thus your research. In addition to having an enormous amount of material at your fingertips, you need to realize that anyone can have a Web site, which means that the material may be creditable or not. Therefore, at the outset, you need to know how to determine the value of your material. The section in Step 3, Evaluating Your Sources, would be helpful for you to read at this point so that you will not be hampered by unreliable material.

CONSIDERING AUDIENCE, PURPOSE, STYLE, AND TONE

As you narrow your subject to a topic, you can make the paper more your own by considering these things: the audience for your paper, the purpose of your paper, and the style and tone of your paper. They will help keep your research focused, and you will be better able to determine how to develop the topic you have chosen.

Keeping Your Audience in Mind

The audience for your paper is a real consideration. If your research is technical, such as researching particular kinds of illnesses from the Persian Gulf War, then your terminology will be more technical than, say, the subject of causes of the Persian Gulf War. In writing about the illnesses that were a result of the war, you would probably use some medical words or terms that the average reader would not understand. If such is the case, you would explain their usages so as not to confuse your audience. On the other hand, if you are writing on a subject of a general nature, you would not be as concerned with detailed explanations.

The bottom line, though, is that it is always important to keep your audience in mind as you write, even if your audience is only your instructor. One good way to do this is to actually think of someone you know who might read your paper and who has no knowledge of your subject. As you are writing, imagine what that person's response might be to what you are writing. To make it even more valid, show your paper in increments to a friend and get his or her reactions. If you do this, you will become more sensitive to your audience. You will write with much better clarity and understanding, because you will know how detailed you need to be and exactly which areas need clarification.

After carefully looking over the investigative questions for Tourette Syndrome, Ellen decided to write her paper on Tourette Syndrome from the standpoint of the effects of the disease on the child; on his or her peers, parents, and family; and how each can cope with the problems associated with Tourette. For this reason, she will not write the paper from a purely scientific standpoint. Although it will incorporate some background and causes of Tourette, the focus will be in another direction. It is easy to see who the audience will be with the paper's taking this angle—the parents of the child with Tourette as well as the child and teachers who deal with children with Tourette Syndrome. This will also affect the tone and style of the paper.

Determining Your Purpose for Writing

The purpose of your paper is also important as it determines the direction of your research, just as knowing the audience of your paper helps you write more clearly. Focusing on the purpose of your paper also helps you determine the format to a great degree, as will be discussed in detail later.

If your paper is meant to be a piece of persuasive writing, you will need to include both sides of the argument—the thesis as well as the antithesis, the pros and the cons. And while you are researching, you may even find yourself with ideas that "straddle the fence," neither pro nor con. It will be your responsibility to see how they can be worked into your paper or whether you can use them at all. Remembering the type of paper you are writing will help you narrow your subject to a workable topic.

The same rule applies with other types of papers—informational, which is developed with the knowledge you have found on a particular subject; comparison and contrast, which uses two similar or contrasting ideas; and cause and effect, which shows the causes of some points and the effects of the causes. The development of papers using these methods will be discussed in Step 8; however, if you know the method you will be using at the time you are doing your research, it will facilitate your search. Another good point to make here is that if you are really researching as you should, you will look for new facts about your subject or those facts that are not generally known rather than resorting to what everyone knows already. After all, that is what research is about—learning things you did not already know. Keeping your purpose in mind as you narrow your subject to a workable topic is important for writing a good paper because it is from your purpose that you usually develop your thesis.

As you have probably discerned, Ellen decided the purpose for her paper on Tourette Syndrome would be to inform parents, family, and teachers what Tourette Syndrome is and how it affects the child. She also decided to incorporate ways each person and/or group could interact for the betterment of the child.

Choosing the Appropriate Style and Tone

The style and tone you use in developing your paper is also a consideration in narrowing the subject. While research papers are more formal than other types of writing, the topic you choose will dictate how formal you will be. For example, a paper that has to do with rap music or radio comedians would be less formal than a paper on the collapse of the Soviet Union. The wording and sentence structure will reflect the difference. With informal writing, your tone would be more conversational, whereas with formal writing your tone would be characterized by a precise and carefully chosen vocabulary and with a more complex sentence structure. With a research paper your tone will be more formal than with personal experience essays or character sketches and the like. The research paper is an academic paper reflecting much time and effort; therefore, it should be more formal than an essay.

Style also involves such things as avoiding contractions and personal pronouns in more formal papers. Because your reader relies on sentence structure and word choice to recognize the tone of your paper, you should use variety in your sentence structure as well as words appropriate to your topic. In addition, it is best to avoid clichés and trite expressions as well as colloquial expressions and shortened forms of words like *exam* for *examination* or *phone* for *telephone*. Being aware of the type of paper you are writing helps determine the focus of your research as well as how you will develop your paper.

The tone of your paper is the attitude you take in your writing. As with style, the tone of your paper is developed early and does not change, whether it is serious and formal or more light-hearted and informal. Usually, the introduction sets the tone for the rest of the paper, which means you need to give careful thought as to how you will introduce your paper. Ellen decided the style and tone of her paper on Tourette Syndrome would be more conversational than formal, since it will be written to help those who have Tourette or who are associated with Tourette.

Narrowing the topic is a very important step because it is the foundation on which to build the rest of your research. It determines the direction of your paper and helps to establish the purpose for your paper as well as the style and content. After you have narrowed your subject to a topic, the next step is to start your research in earnest. Before you do that, however, practice narrowing your subject to a workable topic by doing the following exercises.

EXERCISE 1   General Subject and/or Literary Subject

1. From the subject that you have tentatively chosen for your paper, make a diagram of items or subpoints that you immediately associate with the subject (see page 3).

2. From the diagram, choose one subject you think you might be able to work with and write a list of investigative questions such as the following:
   Who?
   What?
   Where?
   When?
   Why?
   How?

3. After analyzing these questions, choose at least one topic that has emerged.

4. Research the card catalog and the reference section of the library as well as the electronic media to find at least five sources on your topic.

5. Get a folder with pockets on either side that you can use as a portfolio for your work throughout your research. This includes the exercises on this page since they will help you in gathering material for your topic as well as choosing your purpose and style.

EXERCISE 2   Purpose/Style/Tone

1. From the topic you have chosen, write a tentative purpose for your paper.

2. Decide from your purpose whether your paper will be argumentative or expository, that is, informational.

3. Choose the style and tone you think might be most appropriate for your paper. (See page 18 for information on the style and tone chosen for the Tourette paper).

4. Share your findings with a partner to determine whether he or she thinks you have chosen the best style and tone for your paper according to your purpose.

STEP 3

Researching Your Material

Now that you have narrowed your broad subject to a topic you are interested in and feel comfortable with, it is time to start your research. Before you begin, however, it is helpful to plan your research according to the length of time you have been given for your assignment.

PLANNING YOUR TIME

One plan that works well for many students begins at the point where you actually start your research. In other words, your topics have already been narrowed down. While you will need to work within the time frame given by your instructor, whether it is a full semester or one more compressed, the following timetable is suggested.

Tentative Timetable	
Possible thesis statement	End of Week One
Bibliography cards completed	Beginning of Week Two
Note cards completed	End of Week Three
Tentative outline	Beginning of Week Four
Rough draft completed	Beginning of Week Five
Final copy typed and ready to turn in	End of Week Six

This schedule seems to work well; it allows six weeks for you to complete your research paper. You can add more bibliography cards and more note cards if needed, but the bulk of your work should be done within the time given. Without a schedule, the tendency is often to wait until the last minute. When that happens, your paper reflects your haste. It does not have the depth that time allows for you to think about your topic and what it should include. With a schedule, you can pace your work and you will not feel overwhelmed with everything that needs to be done. Six weeks from beginning research to the final draft is usually enough time for thorough research and writing.

You are now ready to begin your research. If your instructor has not given you a schedule to follow, try pacing yourself by using the one provided here. You can be much more successful and less stressed knowing that you are on target with what needs to be done at a particular point.

BEGINNING YOUR RESEARCH

Your school's library is the logical place to begin your research, but many other sources are available. Try your city library or a university library if one is nearby. You may also have a state library in which to do research. In addition, ask your librarian about interlibrary loan programs. These are usually available, especially among libraries in your city and even in your state. If your library has access to this program, your librarian can help you locate material in other libraries so that you can access that bit of difficult information you need to support your paper.

Another way to find sources for your research in an electronically equipped library is to search electronic databases through online services such as InfoTrac SearchBank. It will depend, of course, on what your library is equipped with as to how you will be able to search electronically. As will be discussed later in this Step, some sources on the World Wide Web are more valuable than others, depending on the topic of your research. The important point is that by using these sources, you can immediately retrieve information that is as up-to-date as your daily newspaper.

Understanding the Library

If you are not familiar with the arrangement of your library, trying to find your sources might seem overwhelming. Knowing where and how books are classified is very important. Most libraries, especially school and city libraries, use a method of classifying books called the Dewey Decimal System. Larger libraries, such as university libraries, use the Library of Congress System of classification. Become familiar with both of these systems and you can find material in either situation.

These classification systems are designed to help you find the books or materials you are looking for. Call numbers are on each card in the card catalog and give you information about how to locate the book. For example, if the number on the card catalog is "331 Min" in a library using the Dewey Decimal System, that means the book is in the Social Sciences section of the library. The number 331 represents books on the subject of Labor Economics. The "Min" indicates the author's last name. The book has that call number taped on the spine. Reference books have an "R" before the number. Books located in other special areas also have a letter preceding their call numbers.

The Dewey Decimal System arranges books according to subjects. If you keep this in mind as you do your research, you probably won't even have to ask directions. The system is as follows:

The Dewey Decimal System of Classification

000	General works
100	Philosophy and psychology
200	Religion
300	Social sciences
400	Language
500	Natural sciences and mathematics
600	Technology and applied sciences
700	Fine arts
800	Literature
900	Geography and history

Each category is subdivided according to the number of books in the system. In our example, 331.1 Min indicates a further subdivision of the subject Labor Economics, with 331.1 representing books on the subject of the Labor Force and Market. Further subdivisions may be needed. You will become accustomed to this system as you look for the books you need and as you become more familiar with the card catalog.

As pointed out, most universities use the Library of Congress System of classification. Just as with the Dewey Decimal System, the books are arranged according to subjects. The difference is that the Library of Congress System is based on letters supplemented by numbers. The Library of Congress System uses twenty-one main categories (the letters *I, O, W, X,* and *Y* are not used).

The Library of Congress System of Classification

A	General Works
B	Philosophy, psychology, and religion
C	General history
D	World history
E–F	American history
G	Geography and anthropology
H	Social sciences
J	Political science
K	Law
L	Education
M	Music
N	Fine arts
P	Languages and literature
Q	Science
R	Medicine
S	Agriculture
T	Technology
U	Military science
V	Naval science
Z	Bibliography and library science

Just as with the Dewey Decimal System, categories are further divided under each broad classification. Subdivisions are organized by letters; subclasses are divided by numbers from 1 to 9999. For example, N is Fine Arts; ND is Painting; ND 1700–2495 is Watercolor Painting. This may sound like a lot to remember, but if you bring this manual with you to a library using this system of classification, you should have no trouble finding what you need. Librarians can also help you with your search, and the classification system is usually posted throughout the library.

It is best to find as many books as possible on your topic in the card catalog before you begin searching for your material. On a piece of paper or a card, you might list all of the sources you think you will need. If you find later that some of them are inappropriate, you can simply cross off these titles. Then you will not need to go back and forth to the card catalog to find material.

USING LIBRARY REFERENCE SOURCES

Step 2 explained the two main sources in the library for your research—the card catalog and the reference collection. Even though your library may be equipped with the Internet, and you may be tempted to go immediately to the Web for your research, it would be well for you to explore both the card catalog and reference sources before deciding on the main focus of your research.

Both the electronic catalog and the reference collection may be in printed form or in electronic databases. It is to your advantage, therefore, to understand how to conduct research both manually and electronically. A detailed discussion of searching both traditional and electronic sources is given.

The card catalog, as pointed out in Step 2, is the place most of you will look first. Whether it is an electronic or traditional version, this catalog source contains an index of all books or materials in the library. The electronic version has the advantage of letting you know in a matter of minutes which books are available. Usually the library will also be equipped with a printer so you can print out the information immediately. If not, however, you may simply write down the information you have found for your topic on a card and then begin your research.

Using the Electronic Catalog

The official name for the electronic catalog is *Online Public Access Catalog* (OPAC). Some libraries, however, have formed their own acronyms for OPAC. Find out what is available in your library, because an electronic catalog can make it easier for you to do your research.

The electronic catalog offers the same bibliographic information as the printed catalog. It is also able to search the books in the library not only for the title of the book, the author, and subject matter but also for many topics or keywords within the books themselves. Each item in the book's record is labeled on the screen, which makes it easy for you to research the particular item you need.

FIGURE 3.1

Search menu

```
                Online Public Access Catalog

        Quick Search
        Subject
        Author
        Title
        Author/Title
        All Categories
        Call Number
        More Options . . .                    Space Bar




            Press letter or press arrow and <Return>.
                  Press <F2> for Help.
```

Examples of on-line catalog screens showing the particular areas for research are shown in Figures 3.1–3.6. Figure 3.1 shows the SEARCH MENU of the options that are available for you on the Online Public access Catalog screen.

As you can see, there are many different ways to find the subject you are researching. For the research on Tourette Syndrome, Ellen selected the categories of SUBJECT, TITLE, and ALL CATEGORIES. Figures 3.2–3.6 show what was pulled up on the screen for each category.

Of course, if you already know the name of a particular book or author that you want to research, it is relatively easy to find it by TITLE and/or AUTHOR. However, if you do not have a book to research and are looking instead for a subject, you will find yourself searching in a different way. For example, in order to determine what is available about Tourette Syndrome without knowing the titles of books, Ellen typed in the words *Tourette Syndrome* in the SUBJECT blank. The screen then scanned for that subject and stopped with *Tourette Syndrome*.

FIGURE 3.2

Subject search

```
                          SCAN HEADINGS


            SUBJECT- TOURETTE SYNDROME                    0 Selected

  No.    Heading                                          References
         Toure, Sekou, 1922
   1.       SEE: Toure, Ahmed Sekou, 1922-                     1
         Toure, Sekou, Pres. Guinea, 1922-
   2.       SEE: Toure, Ahmed Sekou, 1922-                     1
   3.    Tourette syndrome                                     6
   4.    Tourette syndrome in children                         1
   5.    Tourette syndrom in children--Patients--United
         States--Biography                                    1
   6.    Tourette syndrome in children--Popular works.        1
  _____
  _  Enter the number of a heading    __ Forward Page         <F5>   _
  _  from the list above.             __ Backward Page        <F6>   _
  _                                   __ Edit Search          <F4>   _
  _                                   __ Review Searches      <F10>  _
  _                                   __ Backup                      _
  _<F1> Start Over      <F2> Help     __ More Options...Space Bar    _
```

From the example in Figure 3.2, you can see that there are a number of listings under the word "Heading" that relate to the subject. These references will help in researching the topic, but in order to find out if these were the only selections in the library, Ellen punched in the SELECT ALL button. This brought up the subject "Tourette Syndrome in Children." This could have been done as well by simply typing in the words "Tourette AND Syndrome AND Children" in the KEYWORD blank; however, since the title is long, the word "Children" would need to be abbreviated for the search.

FIGURE 3.3

Keyword search

```
                  TOURETTE SYNDROME IN CHILDREN

CALL NUMBER:    362.198 H894r
AUTHOR:         Hughes, Susan, 1949-
TITLE:          Ryan--a mother's story of her hyperactive/
                Tourette syndrome child/Susan Hughes
IMPRINT:        Duarte, CA: Hope Press, c1990. viii, 153p.; 21 cm.
SUBJECT 1:      Hughes, Ryan James, 1979--Health
SUBJECT 2:      Tourette syndrome in children--Patients--United
                States--Biography
SUBJECT 3:      Hyperactive Children--United States--Biography
NOTE 1:         Includes bibiographical references and index
OCLC NO:        20933346


_ Select an Option              __ Display Summary          _
_                               __ Print            <F5>    _
_                               __ Previous Record          _
                                __ Forward Page     <F5>    _
                                __ Backward Page    <F6>    _
_<F1> Start Over    <F2> Help   __ More Options...Space Bar _
```

As shown in Figure 3.3, inputting the phrase "children AND tourette AND syndrome" led to Susan Hughes' book, *Tourette Syndrome in Children*. That refines the subject by giving a definite place to do research. The next step could logically go in two directions—find the book by title or by author. Figure 3.4 conveys the way the title entry is displayed with the screen's showing a full record of *Ryan: A Mother's Story of Her Hyperactive/Tourette Syndrome Child*.

FIGURE 3.4

Title search

```
        TITLE=RYAN A MOTHERS STORY OF HER HYPERACTIV>        0 Selected

   No.  Heading                                          References

    1.  Rx for your vegetable garden/                          1
    2.  Rx: prescription for murder/                           1
    3.  Rx, the Christian love treatment/                      1
    4.  Ryan--a mother's story of her hyperactive/Tourette     1
        syndrome child/
    5.  Ryan Airport master plan/                              1
    6.  Ryan, Gregory.                                         1
    7.  Ryan rides back/                                       1
    8.  Ryan White.                                            1
   _____
   _ Enter the number of a heading   __ Forward Page      <F5>   _
   _ from the list above.            __ Backward Page     <F6>   _
   _                                 __ Edit Search       <F4>   _
   _                                 __ Review Searches   <F10>  _
   _                                 __ Backup                   _
   _<F1> Start Over    <F2> Help     __ More Options...Space Bar _
```

As you can see, the title search includes many entries beginning with the letter *R*. The book, *Ryan: A Mother's Story of Her Hyperactive/Tourette Syndrome Child*, is listed as number 4. In order to get the detailed information with the call number of the book, it would be necessary to highlight the entry for the book, which will give you the call number and other information similar to Figure 3.3. The detailed text description that then appears on the screen will contain several clues to help you determine if this is the source you need. It will also point you to additional bibliographies and indexes that may be helpful. It will be up to you to check them out see if they might be beneficial to you in your research.

FIGURE 3.5

Author entry

```
       AUTHOR=HUGHES SUSAN                              0 Selected

No.    Heading                                         References

 1.    Hughes-Stanton, Penelope                            1
 2.    Hughes, Stephen.                                    1
 3.    Hughes, Stephen Ormsby, 1924-                       1
 4.    Hughes, Stevie.                                     1
*5.    Hughes, Susan, 1949-                                1
 6.    Hughes, Susan, 1960-                                6
       Hughes, Sylvia
 7.    SEE: Plath, Sylvia.                                11
 8.    Hughes, Talbot.                                     1
_____
_ Select another number or      __ Display Brief Records <F9>  _
_ select an option-------->     __ Forward Page          <F5>  _
_                               __ Backward Page          <F6>  _
_                               __ Edit Search            <F4>  _
_                               __ Deselect All                 _
_<F1> Start Over    <F2> Help   __ More Options... Space Bar   _
```

If you also want to search using the AUTHOR entry, you will find a screen similar to the Title screen, except that it will give a list of authors with the last name of Hughes, as shown in Figure 3.5.

In order to get the full information of the book's availability, SUSAN HUGHES was highlighted as shown in Figure 3.6. As you see, there are two Susan Hugheses listed. The date beside each name indicates the date of birth. Since you already know from the keyword search that the date of birth of Susan Hughes, author of *Ryan: A Mother's Story of Her Hyperactive/Tourette Syndrome Child,* is 1949, you will choose that Susan Hughes. You can see from the screen how many copies are available and the status—where they are located and whether they are checked out.

FIGURE 3.6

Copy availability

```
    AUTHOR= HUGHES SUSAN

  AUTHOR:              Hughes, Susan, 1949-
  TITLE:               Ryan--a mother's story of her hyperactive/
                       Tourette syndrome child/Susan Hughes
  IMPRINT:             Duarte, CA: Hope Press, c1990.

  Location             Call Number                Status
  Main Library         362.198 H894r              On Shelf
  Jones Creek          362.198 H894r              On Shelf
  Scotlandville        362.198 H894r              On Shelf

  _____

  _ Select an option          __ Display Full Record   <F7>  _
  _                            __ Display Summary             _
  _                            __ Review Searches      <F10>  _
  _                            __ Help                  <F2>  _
  _                            __ Backup                      _
  _<F1> Start Over   <F2> Help __ More Options...   Space Bar _
```

As you research your topic using the electronic catalog, you can easily see the advantages of the electronic method over the traditional method of research. However, both the electronic and traditional card catalogs have basically the same information and accomplish the same results.

Using the Traditional Card Catalog

The traditional card catalog contains cards listing information about every book in the library, both fiction and nonfiction. There are three types of cards for each book: (1) author card, (2) title card, and (3) subject card. All three types of cards contain the same information, but they are filed according to one of the three headings: AUTHOR, TITLE, or SUBJECT.

The traditional card catalog is set up in alphabetical order with a label on each drawer. The basic information on each card in the card catalog is (1) call number, (2) subject, (3) author's name, (4) author's year of birth, (5) year of death if author is deceased, (6) title of book, (7) publisher, (8) copyright date, (9) number of pages, (10) illustrations, if any, and (11) other information, such as maps, annotations, tracing line, and Library of Congress number or Dewey Decimal classification.

Call numbers of fiction books contain the letter "F" and usually the first three letters of the author's last name. Story collections are found in some libraries with the letters "SC" and letters from the author's last name. Each library may use its own classification system for story collections, which means they may not all be alike. Browse through the library if you need to use the story collection and find the classification system it uses. Better yet, ask the librarian.

Samples of the author card, title card, and subject card from the traditional card catalog are shown in Figures 3.7–3.9. These cards concern Tourette Syndrome in Children because that is the focus of the research paper included in Appendix A.

FIGURE 3.7

Author card

362.198 H894r	**Hughes, Susan, 1949–**
	Ryan: A Mother's Story of Her Hyperactive/Tourette Syndrome Child
	Duarte, CA: Hope Press, c1990
	viii, 153 p. : 21 cm.
Subject 1:	Hughes, Ryan James, 1979—Health
Subject 2:	Tourette Syndrome in Children—Patients— United States—Biography
Subject 3:	Hyperactive Children—United States—Biography Includes bibliographical references and index
Note 1:	Includes bibliographical references and index

FIGURE 3.8

Title card

362.198 H894r	**Ryan: A Mother's Story of Her Hyperactive/Tourette Syndrome Child**
	Hughes, Susan, 1949–
	Duarte, CA: Hope Press, c1990
	viii, 153 p. : 21 cm.
Subject 1:	Hughes, Ryan James, 1979—Health
Subject 2:	Tourette Syndrome in Children—Patients— United States—Biography
Subject 3:	Hyperactive Children—United States—Biography Includes bibliographical references and index
Note 1:	Includes bibliographical references and index

362.198 H894r	**Tourette Syndrome in Children**
	Hughes, Susan, 1949–
	Ryan: A Mother's Story of Her Hyperactive/Tourette Syndrome Child/Susan Hughes
	Duarte, CA: Hope Press, c1990 viii, 153 p. : 21 cm.
Subject 1:	Hughes, Ryan James, 1979—Health
Subject 2:	Tourette Syndrome in Children—Patients—United States—Biography
Subject 3:	Hyperactive Children—United States—Biography
Note 1:	Includes bibliographical references and index

Using the Reference Collection

The reference collection is another time-saver. Professors and experts throughout the United States are paid to research and compile material so that you can have it at your fingertips. After you learn how to use this part of the library, you will understand how valuable it is.

Listed here are sources included in the reference collection with a short explanation after the list. Many of these sources are available in both print and electronic format.

1. Indexes
2. Literary sources
3. Ready reference sources
4. Specialized encyclopedias and dictionaries
5. Electronic sources

Printed Indexes. Today most periodical indexes are published in an electronic format; however, for many years, the foremost printed periodical index has been *The Reader's Guide to Periodical Literature* or just *Periodical Index*. It indexes general references of articles from approximately 130 magazines and serves as a guide to these periodicals. It is published twice monthly and has a bound cumulative edition published annually. As in the card catalog, articles can be found under either author entry or subject entry. If you use this source, you will usually search from the latest issue and work backward, because you want the most recent source of information for your topic. If magazines in your library are not kept in open stacks, take the information you have found to the librarian, who will get the magazine for you from the stack room.

In addition to the *Periodical Index* already noted, there are other indexes in which you might find exactly what you want. The Wilson Company publishes periodical indexes on education, library science, and agriculture. Other indexes commonly used in schools include *Granger's Index of Poetry* and *The Short Story Index,* as well as other specialized indexes.

Electronic Indexes. As noted earlier, many electronic indexes are also available in the printed format and are frequently found in schools and other libraries. Some of the electronic indexes most used include *Magazine Article Summaries, CD-ROM,* and databases such as SearchBank, InfoTrac, and GaleNet which offer summaries of information about authors, biographies, science, poetry, and so forth. These then point you to larger works to explore. It isn't hard to see the many advantages of the electronic indexes. They can provide you with a comprehensive listing of articles immediately, thus speeding your research. Many electronic resources also provide either abstracts or full-text material ready to be printed, which makes your research faster and more efficient.

Figure 3.10 shows how to research using the electronic source InfoTrac. As you can see from the screen, InfoTrac offers a plethora of databases from which you can research. Note, though, that some of the databases are indexes that in themselves are not sources for specific information; they are simply sites for further research. The databases offered by InfoTrac include:

Gen'l Reference Ctr (Magazine Index)
Health Reference Center-Academic
General BusinessFile ASAP
Expanded Academic ASAP
National Newspaper Index
Computer Database

FIGURE 3.10

Electronic index source—InfoTrac

I N F O T R A C

SearchBank

Please select a database to search

Gen'l Reference Ctr (Magazine Index) 1980 - Jun 1999
Use this general interest database to search magazines, reference books, and newspapers for information on current events, popular culture, the arts and sciences, etc.

Health Reference Center-Academic 1995 - Jun 1999
Use this database to find article on: Fitness, Pregnancy, Medicine, Nutrition, Diseases, Public Health, Occupational Health & Safety, Alcohol and Drug abuse, HMOs, Prescription Drugs, etc. The material contained in this database is intended for informational purposes only. Disclaimer.

General BusinessFile ASAP 1980 - Jun 1999
Use this database to research all business and management topics. Includes directory listings for over 150,000 companies as well as investment analysts' reports on major companies and industries.

Expanded Academic ASAP 1980 - Jun 1999
Use this database to find information on: Astronomy, Religion, Law, History, Psychology, Humanities, Current Events, Sociology, Communications and the General Sciences.

National Newspaper Index 1996 - Jun 1999
Use this database to find information on: Current Events, Lifestyle, Biographies, Sports, Economics, Consumer Products, World Affairs, Public Health, Business Trends, Entertainment and Travel.

Computer Database 1996 - Jun 1999
Use this database to find computer-related product introductions, news, and reviews in areas such as hardware, software, electronics, engineering, communications and the application of technology.

http://web7.searchbank.com/itw/session/129/982/30974804w3/

After choosing Health Reference Center—Academic, the next step was to type the phrase "Tourette and syndrome and children," and then hit SEARCH. From Figure 3.11, you can see a number of articles pertaining to Tourette Syndrome and children. Ellen chose to view the abstract of an essay entitled "Stimulant Medication Withdrawal During Long-Term Therapy in Children With Comorbid Attention-Deficit Hyperactivity Disorder and Chronic Multiple Tic Disorder" published in *Pediatrics*, April 1999, and written by Edith E. Nolan, Kenneth D. Gadow, and Joyce Sprafkin. The abstract gave the main ideas of the article in a shortened version, but since the full text was given along with the abstract, she could easily determine if the article would be useful for researching Tourette Syndrome. Figure 3.12 shows the screen of the abstract and full text of the article searched about Tourette Syndrome.

In addition to the online electronic database InfoTrac, other databases also offer valuable information concerning periodicals. Many publishers offer these electronic research sources full-text with the ability to print all or parts of the articles. These include periodical and/or newspaper coverage. Examples of these sources include:

1. GaleNet, which provides information from periodicals on different topics and offers text viewing and retrieval choices.
2. EBSCO's Magazine Article Summaries (MAS), which offers full-text coverage of over 75 periodical titles and annotated coverage of hundreds more.
3. *Proquest*, which offers a service similar to MAS.
4. NEWSBANK, which provides newspaper articles on selected high-interest topics from major newspapers around the United States.

Literary Sources. If your research paper is to be of a literary nature, you will want to search that part of the library where reference books are kept. Some books carry information about the author and the work, while others are primarily biographical. Of course, it depends on how well equipped your library is, but the following list offers some research direction for the works themselves. Note, though, this list is not all-inclusive; it should be used only as examples of where to look.

1. Magill's *Survey of Contemporary Literature*
2. Magill's *1300 Critical Evaluations of Novels and Plays*
3. Magill's *Survey of Science Fiction and Literature*
4. *Masterpieces of African-American Literature*
5. *Oxford Companion to English Literature* (which includes English and American Literature—Literature from the English language)
6. *Oxford Companion to African American Literature*

FIGURE 3.11

Articles available from InfoTrac

INFOTRAC
SearchBank

Citations 1 to 17
Key Words: (Tourette and syndrome and children)

Stimulant Medication Withdrawal During Long-term Therapy in Children With Comorbid Attention-Deficit Hyperactivity Disorder and Chronic Multiple Tic Disorder.
Edith E. Nolan, Kenneth D. Gadow, Joyce Sprafkin.
    Pediatrics April 1999 v103 i4 p730(1)
    View text and retrieval choices

B lymphocyte antigen D8/17 and repetitive behaviors in autism. Eric Hollander, Ginal DelGiudice-Asch, Lorraine Simon, James Schmeidler, Charles Cartwright, Concetta M. DeCaria, Jee Kwon, Charlotte Cunningham-Rundles, Floresta Chapman, John B. Zabriskie.
    American Journal of Psychiatry Feb 1999 v 156 i2 p317(4)
    View abstract and retrieval choices

Tourette's associated with comorbid conditions.
    The Brown University Child and Adolescent Behavior Letter
Feb 1999 v15 i2 p3(1)
    View text and retrieval choices

Clues about Tourette's Syndrome.
    The Science Teacher Sep 1998 v65 n6 p14(1)
    View abstract and retrieval choices

Course of tic severity in Tourette syndrome: the first two decades. James F. Leckman, Heping Zhang, Amy Vitale, Fatima Lahnin, Kimberly Lynch, Colin Bondi, Young-shin Kim, Bradley S. Peterson.
    Pediatrics July 1998 v102 n1 p14(6)
    View text and retrieval choices

Pediatric autoimmune neuropsychiatric disorders associated with streptococcal infections: clinical description of the first 50 cases. Susan E. Swedo, Henrietta L. Leonard, Marjorie Garvey, Barbara Mittleman, Albert J. Allen, Susan Perlmutter, Sara Dow, Jason Zamkoff, Billinda K. Dubbert, Lorraine Lougee.
    American Journal of Psychiatry Feb 1998 v155 n2 p264(8)
    View abstract and retrieval choices

http://web3.searchbank.com/itw/session/53/226/30973720w3/sig!1

FIGURE 3.12

Full text of article from InfoTrac

I N F O T R A C
SearchBank

Pediatrics, April 1999 v103 i4 p730(1)

Stimulant Medication Withdrawal During Long-term Therapy in Children With Comorbid Attention-Deficit Hyperactivity Disorder and Chronic Multiple Tic Disorder. *Edith E. Nolan; Kenneth D. Gadow; Joyce Sprafkin.*

Abstract: Withdrawal of stimulant medication does not appear to increase the severity of tics in children with attention deficit hyperactivity disorder (ADHD) and verbal or motor tics. Tics are brief, uncontrolled movements or utterances. Researchers evaluated 19 children after they stopped taking methylphenidate (Ritalin) or dextroamphetamine for ADHD. Withdrawal of the medication did not result in an increase in tic frequency or severity.

Objectives. In this study we examined changes in attention-deficit hyperactivity disorder behaviors and motor and vocal tics during withdrawal from long-term maintenance therapy with stimulant medication.

Methods. Subjects were 19 children with attention-deficit hyperactivity disorder and chronic tic disorder who had received methylphenidate (n = 17) or dextroamphetamine (n = 2) for a minimum of 1 year. Children were switched to placebo under double-blind conditions. Treatment effects were assessed by using direct observations of child behavior in a simulated (clinic-based) classroom and behavior rating scales completed by parents and clinician.

Results. There was no change (group data) in the frequency of severity of motor tics or vocal tics during the placebo condition compared with maintenance dose of stimulant medication (ie. no evidence of tic exacerbation while receiving medication or of a withdrawal reaction). There was no evidence of tic exacerbation in the evening as a rebound effect. Treatment with the maintenance dose was also associated with behavioral improvement in attention-deficit hyperactivity disorder behaviors, indicating continued efficacy.

Conclusions. Abrupt withdrawal of stimulant medication in children receiving long-term maintenance therapy does not appear to result in worsening of tic frequency or severity. Nevertheless, these findings do not preclude the possibility of drug withdrawal reactions in susceptible individuals. Pediatrics 1999:103:730-737; attention-deficit hyperactivity disorder, methylphenidate, aggression, tic disorder, Tourette's syndrome.

http://web3.searchbank.com/itw/session/206/625/30973044w3/19!xrn_1_0_A54432352

If you also want to research an author's life, some of the reference sources that are entirely of a biographical nature include the following:

1. *Dictionary of American Biography*
2. *Dictionary of Literary Biography*
3. *Discovering Authors*
4. *Current Biography*
5. *American Writers*
6. *Contemporary American Authors*
7. *Living Authors*
8. *Twentieth Century Authors*

In addition to biographical information about authors, some of these reference works contain critiques of the writers' works. Similar books are also available for British writers and world authors. The literary biographical reference section is often one of the best places to find material about a literary topic.

Other sources include *Master Plots* or *Book Review Digest* which offer summaries of works as well as excerpts from reviews others have written about the books and short critiques of the works. If your research time is short, you may find that book review summaries are invaluable in giving you some insight into your topic. By reading them before you read the books—if that is the focus of your paper—these overall views can help you determine the direction you want to take. Making these summaries the primary source of your research, though, is prohibited. They are only to be used as springboards for further research.

Of course, many of these resources are also available on electronic databases such as GaleNet and InfoTrac. For example, Gale offers in its *Literature Resource Center* biographical, bibliographical, and contextual information integrating content from 90,000 entries in *Contemporary Authors*, *Contemporary Literary Criticism*, and *Dictionary of Literary Biography*. This makes GaleNet a one-stop resource for information on authors, their works, and criticism of their works. In addition, the World Wide Web offers an online database, Biography.com, in which more than 20,000 notable people, past and present, can be found.

Poem Finder on the Web is another impressive database with full-text poems, citations, and source references, indexing poetry from 3,000 anthologies, 4,500 single-author works, and 5,000 periodicals. Other databases of a literary nature are becoming increasingly available. Which ones to select from will be a problem rather than not having enough material from which to choose.

Ready References. If you are just beginning your research, encyclopedias are a good source to use, but be careful not to confine yourself only to an encyclopedia. Encyclopedias, by their very nature, must cover so many subjects that they cannot contain the in-depth coverage you need in your research. They should only be used as a beginning point—a place to start finding out something about your subject. It is a good idea to branch out into other works, no matter what you are researching. Allow encyclopedias only to direct you to additional material; do not use them as the primary source for your paper.

A number of different encyclopedias can be found in most school libraries. They are aimed at different audiences, which means you should choose the one most appropriate for you. The depth of your subject will help you decide which encyclopedias can best handle your research. Most schools have *World Book, Colliers, Britannica,* and *Americana,* while some will also have *Columbia Encyclopedia, Chamber's Encyclopedia,* and the *New International Encyclopedia.*

Many encyclopedias are also found on CD-ROM, such as *Multimedia Encyclopedia* by World Book, *Grolier's Electronic Encyclopedia* (Academic American), *Compton's Multi-Media Encyclopedia, Encarta, Encyclopedia Americana,* and *Britannica Instant Research System.* These encyclopedias can print all or parts of the articles found on any subject.

Specialized Encyclopedias. There are a number of single- and multiple-volume works that pertain to different occupations, such as *The Guide to the History of Science and Space Encyclopedia.* Another excellent source is *Taylor's Encyclopedia of Government Officials—Federal and State,* published every other year, that provides invaluable information for social studies research. There are even sports encyclopedias for those who need to research sports figures or a particular sport. If you are researching a specialized subject, you can probably find just the right encyclopedia you need pertaining to that topic.

You may also need a general dictionary for information of a broad nature. However, more specialized dictionaries are often needed. *The Dictionary of Literary Terms,* for example, is helpful if you need to research a literary term, such as *satire* or *symbolism.* There are also dictionaries on every subject, as well as almanacs, concordances, yearbooks, and books of lists, such as *The Guinness Book of World Records,* which provide specialized information. On-line Dictionaries is a Web site that is also available, and it includes general dictionaries as well as specialized dictionaries.

Other Electronic Sources. Some information has already been given about electronic sources, such as *Magazine Articles Summaries CD-ROM;* GaleNet, which provides information about a number of databases from which to search; InfoTrac, which includes Books in Print; encyclopedias on CD-ROM; and electronic newspaper and periodical sources. In addition, there are other electronic sources, usually in a CD-ROM format. Most can be researched by using keywords, and all or parts of their articles can be printed. The list that follows describes some of these sources and the information they cover.

Subject-Related Sources

1. *McGraw Hill Multimedia Encyclopedia of Science and Technology.* Full-text encyclopedia.
2. *U.S. History on CD-ROM.* Full-text coverage of more than 125 well-known books on American history.
3. *Discovering Authors: 300 Biographies.* Full-text coverage of biographical, general information, career, writing, and critical sources.
4. *The Columbia Granger's Poetry Index* (CD-ROM). Indexes 80,000 poems by author, title, first line, subject, and the anthologies in which they are indexed.
5. *Scribner Writer Series.* Full-text coverage of American writers, British writers, and others.

Internet Service Providers

Today, many commercial online service providers offer access to the Internet. Being online simply means that the information is constantly being updated and delivered to the computer by a modem hooked up to telephone lines. The services are fee-based, in other words, they are not free. Many of these service providers offer a set number of hours per month for a set fee; others charge a flat rate per month.

Some of the providers that you are probably familiar with are given here. However, numerous other companies offer access through 800 numbers. Simply dial the number, and you are online.

1. America Online (AOL)
2. AT&T
3. Compuserve
4. MCI
5. Microsoft Network
6. TCI

What these service providers do is give you access to the Internet, the world's information superhighway. Also known as the World Wide Web, it continues to grow every day. Perhaps you have a personal computer at home with access to the Internet or access to one of these services at school. Use this valuable resource, but use it correctly. As will be discussed later in this chapter, it is very important to evaluate your sources from the Web to be sure that they contain documented, copyrighted material.

Figure 3.13 shows how the subject Tourette Syndrome was researched using the internet service provider America Online. It shows the screen with the word *Tourette* typed into the keyword search bar.

FIGURE 3.13

Screen showing AOL search

As you can see, the search was made through *Health* with the subheading *Conditions and Diseases*. Displayed were the matching sites. You will notice that the first four sites have "100%" listed to the left of the title. This means they fully fit the criteria of the search. These sites are all from associations and organizations that offer support and information to people with Tourette Syndrome (TS), so they would be valuable for the research paper on Tourette. Some 190 other findings also appeared that could be researched simply by highlighting the entry selected.

If you want to use the World Wide Web after going online, it is necessary to know what to do. There are two primary ways to use the Web: (1) use the address of what you are looking for and (2) use a search engine. The problem with using an address is that often you do not know the exact address to put in the search box on the screen, which makes it necessary to use a search engine. It would be helpful, then, for you to know exactly what a search engine is and how to use it.

Search Engines

A search engine, put simply, is just a way to find things on the Net. Many search engines are free Web-based tools; others have a minimal cost. Two kinds of search tools—directories and indexes—are used with the Internet. Keeping in mind the difference between a directory and an index will help your research.

Think of it this way: A search engine directory is similar to a book's table of contents, which is divided into headings and subheadings. These divisions help narrow your focus in the book so that you can find what you are looking for more easily. A search engine also has categories and subcategories that help narrow your search. These categories point to links that will further your research.

On the other hand, a search engine index is much like the index of a book. For example, if you wanted to find where something particular is, you would go to the back of the book and look in the index. That is what a search engine index does. It collects millions of items, extracts keywords from them, and makes a big list. That makes it possible for you to refine your search more quickly; however, the key to finding exactly what you need is knowing the best words for your search. If you have difficulty in locating what you are looking for, perhaps you are searching in the wrong way. For example, use lowercase letters completely (except with the first letter of a proper name) unless your search engine is case-insensitive, which means the upper- or lowercase letters make no difference. If you are searching for a phrase, such as Tourette Syndrome, put quotes around the words. Also, if you are searching for words that do not normally appear together, use + and – to indicate words that must or must not appear. An illustration might be tourette + syndrome + children. By using the word *children* with *tourette* and *syndrome*, you will limit your search to children. If you were searching for Tourette Syndrome as it relates to adults, you would put a minus before the word children. That would limit your search, then, to adults. After you have found the material you are looking for, you will see that much of it is full-text, an advantage allowing you to pick and choose what you need.

Although there are many search tools, the ones listed here are those used most in the academic setting. The lists, however, keep changing, so keep abreast of the latest directories and indexes for the most current research tools. The address, or URL (location), of each search engine is also given.

Directories

1. Yahoo!—http://www.yahoo.com
2. Argus Clearinghouse—http://www.clearinghouse.net
3. Virtual Library—http:www.w3.org/vl
4. Galaxy—http://www.einet.net
5. Snap—http://snap.com

Indexes

1. AltaVista—http://altavista.digital.com
2. Northern Light—http://northernlight.com
3. Excite—http://www.excite.com
4. HotBot—http://www.hotbot.com
5. InfoSeek—http://www.infoseek.com
6. Lycos—http://www.lycos.com

Some schools use one or more of these entirely, and some indexes are linked with certain directories; for example, AltaVista is often linked with Yahoo!. The advantage in such a case is that Yahoo! can be used as a directory for finding information while AltaVista is the index for the information. It is also not necessary to get out of Yahoo! to go to AltaVista, an additional plus.

If you are really having trouble finding exactly what you want using the directory you have, there is still another way to search: use a metasearch engine. A metasearch engine allows you to have access to to the databases of more than a single search engine or directory. Because of the efficiency and speed of search, many libraries with high levels of Internet usage requiring computer time to be scheduled and limited direct students to metasearch tools. Check with your librarian to see if your library is equipped with a metasearch engine. The list here is not a comprehensive listing of the metasearch engines available, but these are rated highly.

Metasearch Engines

1. ByteSearch—http://www.bytesearch.com
2. Mamma—http://www.mamma.com
3. MetaCrawler—http://www.go2net.com
4. ProFusion—http://www.profusion.com
5. SavvySearch—http://www.savvysearch.com
6. Copernic—http://www.copernic.com
7. Dogpile—http://www.dogpile.com

As you can see from the printed and electronic sources given in this step, the field of sources for you to research is wide open. Step 3 is very important because it shows multiple sources you can use for your research. It directs you to information on almost any subject you need to research. Now it is up to you!

As you look in these sources, however, you will need to record the information for your bibliography or source cards that will be used later in your Works Cited page. Exactly what you need to record is discussed in Step 4.

Before you go to Step 4, however, one more thing needs to be stressed, and that is how to go about evaluating your resources for the Internet. The cyberspace age has brought with it unlimited information from around the world, and that in itself is also one of its drawbacks. As you may have discovered if you have access to the World Wide Web, anyone can create his or her own Web page and publish anything on it, whether it is credible or just trash. Therefore, you need to be aware of the sources for your material and whether they can be authenticated. Some guidelines follow that will help you determine if your sources are acceptable.

Evaluating Your Sources

There are several ways to figure out whether your sources are credible or not.

Address

The very first thing you should do when you bring up an article on the Internet is to check the source. That means to look for the address. One way of identification is to look at the last few letters in the URL or address, which is called the *domain name* or the location of the account on the Internet.

Those you will usually find are listed here:

1. com—commercial
2. edu—education
3. gov—government
4. mil—military
5. net—network
6. org—organization (sometimes nonprofit)

If you know the domain address, it will help you determine the source of the article and may even help you check its reliability. For example, if the domain address is "edu," the information came from a university and should be educational. Of course, a student's homepage may also have "edu" as a part of his or her homepage address. If it is "com," it is commercial. That means the material may be aimed toward selling you something or may be from an individual. After all, it is not difficult to get your own Web site.

Author

After you have looked at the domain name, your next step is to determine who the author is, what his or her credentials are, what the educational backgrounds and experience in the field are, how recent the material is, and whether it is a primary or secondary source. In order to determine who the author is and his or her credentials, background, and experience, go back to the file you have downloaded. For example, Ellen downloaded the article, "Recognition and Management of Tourette's Syndrome and Tic Disorders," from InfoTrac SearchBank.com. The article was written by Mohammed M. Bagheri, Jacob Kerbeshian, and Larry Burd. A list of references follows the article with the doctors' names, indicating they have done much research in the field of Tourette. The article itself was from *American Family Physician*, dated April 15, 1999. We can assume from this information, then, that the article definitely has credibility.

Primary versus Secondary

In order to determine whether a source is primary or secondary, you will need to look at where the material came from. For example, the article from *Pediatrics* (Figure 3.12) was taken from a presentation to the American Academy of Pediatrics by Edith Nolan, Kenneth Gadow, and Joyce Sprafkin, and the date is 1999. It also bears the seal of the American Academy of Pediatrics, which in itself gives approval for the study. The article is full-text with an abstract at the beginning by the authors who are the primary source; *Pediatrics* is the secondary source. Since the article is copyrighted by the American Academy of Pediatrics, 1999, it bears credibility and shows the recency of the study. In addition, it means that *Pediatrics* will be careful to print the material exactly as it is given. This example shows how important it is to check sources because outdated material is not as valuable as newer material in some research. It demonstrates as well that the very first thing you should do is to determine if the material is valid.

While you are checking sources, you need to bear in mind that if you are doing sophisticated research that demands critical thinking and analyzing information relevant to your topic, you will want to be sure you have primary sources. An excellent source you will want to explore is through the Library of Congress Web site (http://lcweb.loc.gov). For example, authentic primary sources are available through the Library of Congress American Memory Web site as well as the American Memory collection. These online primary source collections have resources that include African American Perspectives, Architecture and Interior Design for 20th Century America, Poet at Work, Jackie Robinson and Other Baseball Highlights, 1860s–1960s, "Votes for Women" Suffrage Pictures, 1850–1920, as well as many, many more.

For instance, if you were interested in researching Alexander Graham Bell's notebook entry of March 10, 1876, you could read how Bell describes his successful experiment with the telephone. The words he spoke to his assistant: "Mr. Watson—come here—I want to see you" have more meaning when you can see the actual entry.

As you can visualize such incidents of first-hand accounts, it is easy to see the value of having these primary sources available through The Library of

Congress Web site. Your paper will be much more interesting than reading what someone else had to say about Bell's invention, which would be a secondary source.

The point is that, first of all, you need to have an acceptable source. After you have made that determination, continue your evaluation by asking yourself the following questions:

1. Does the resource show bias—leaning toward one ideology to the exclusion of others?

2. Is the resource promoting something or is it providing information and facts that can be checked for validity?

3. Is the author or organization promoting the material credible? Can you check their resources or are they given? (If not, you may be looking at only one person's viewpoint to the exclusion of others.)

4. Is the information verifiable?

5. Is the information up-to-date or is it static (at a standstill)?

6. Is the text clear and well written with a particular audience and purpose evident?

7. Does the material do what it aims to do according to the title and/or subject of the article?

8. What do other reviewers say about the material and the resource?

Reviews

One of the best ways to determine whether a source is credible is to see what reviewers have said about the material. In that way, you have some idea of whether the information has been used or tried and how valuable it is.

In searching for an evaluation of what is found on Tourette Syndrome, Ellen found it interesting that Susan Hughes had written a sequel to the book, *Ryan: A Mother's Story of Her Hyperactive/Tourette Syndrome Child*. The sequel, *What Makes Ryan Tick?*, covers the adolescent years and picks up where the other book left off. Two reviewers had reviewed the book, one was a CNN senior correspondent and the other was the chief of child adolescent services, Ventura County Mental Health.

Figure 3.14 shows the title page of the book *What Makes Ryan Tick?* on the Internet. Because of the information given, the material will clearly be useful in the research paper on Tourette Syndrome.

Figure 3.15 shows the two reviews. As you can see, they clearly indicate that Susan Hughes has not only told a heart-wrenching story but also has done something for the betterment of mankind through her determination to find the best for her son. Because both reviewers have similar feelings about her book, there is more credibility, especially since one review is written from a professional point of view while the other is written from a human interest point of view.

FIGURE 3.14

Book page from *What Makes Ryan Tick?*

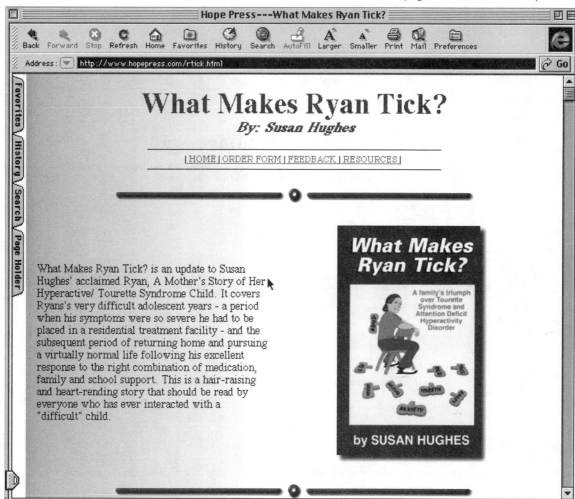

Of course, evaluating this source by what reviewers have said does not satisfy the complete criteria for evaluating the source. Validity is established, though, because Susan Hughes is the mother of Ryan, and she is the one who encountered the problems with the medical and educational professions. She lived with Ryan every day and saw his erratic behavior compounded by a lack of understanding on the part of some in the medical and educational fields. She provides further credibility by documenting everything that happened to her son, both good and bad.

While this source is fairly easy to evaluate using what the reviewers have said and because of Susan Hughes' first-hand experience, you need to understand that, while the Internet provides immediate information, much of it is not academic and thus is not what you are looking for in real research. Be aware of this so that you will not accept what you find without delving into whether it is acceptable material. The bottom line is that anyone can put

FIGURE 3.15

Review of the book *What Makes Ryan Tick?*

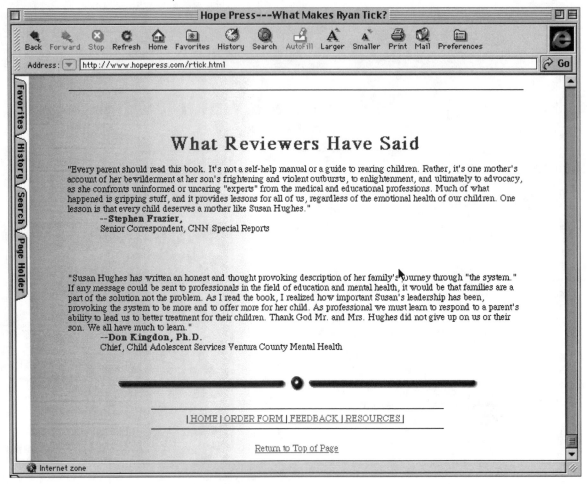

material on the Internet, so it is up to you to be your own sleuth and determine its authenticity.

In order to assimilate the information from this chapter and put it into practice, try the following exercises given for evaluating your sources and using the library.

EXERCISE 1

Evaluating Your Internet Sources

1. Look up an article on the Internet concerning the subject you have decided to research. Give the primary source of information for the article as well as the secondary source, if there is a secondary source available. Write down the domain address and determine what kind of source it is. Evaluate the source according to the relevancy of the subject and the date it was compiled.

2. Evaluate the article you looked up on the Internet according to the eight questions on page 46 concerning how to evaluate your research. Record this information to be discussed in class.

3. Find the subject you have chosen both by keyword and by one of the search engines available. Write down two sources you could use for your research from these two methods of research. Record the information about both of them so that you can use it later in writing your paper.

EXERCISE 2   ## Using the Classification System of Your Library

1. Find a cookbook or a book on car racing using either the Dewey Decimal System or the Library of Congress System. Write down its title and the call number.

2. Find a book on abortion or euthanasia and write down its title and call number.

3. Write down the title and the call number of a book of poems by your favorite poet.

4. Write down the title and call number of a book about a famous athlete.

EXERCISE 3   ## Using the Electronic Catalog

1. Using the electronic card catalog, find three resources for the topic you narrowed down in Step 2, preferably searching by SUBJECT, TITLE, and AUTHOR.

2. Print at least one page from this selection.

3. Write down the call numbers for these three sources.

4. Locate the three sources, using the call numbers you wrote down.

EXERCISE 4   ## Using Other Reference Sources

1. Choose a subject, such as the Indy 500 or your favorite singer. By using one of the electronic sources, write down information on at least three magazines articles.

2. Using the traditional or electronic encyclopedia, find an article about the "least tern," a bird that is almost extinct. Record where you found it and where the least tern makes its home.

3. From an electronic periodical index, search for magazine articles on "bionomediation," which is a solution to waste pollution. Record where you found it and what the solution is.

Preparing Source Cards or Bibliography Cards

In recent years the term *source card*, instead of *bibliography card*, has become popular to identify the references used. *Source card* is a better term because it says exactly what it means—sources used in your paper. For example, if you use five different sources in your paper, you would list five sources on your Works Cited page, because the Works Cited page is exactly what its name implies—those works that are cited in the paper. If you do not cite a work, that means you did not use the work.

While a long list of works may look impressive to the untrained eye, the instructor who reads your paper can recognize that you have merely listed works and not used them. That is an unacceptable practice.

COMPILING COMPLETE SOURCE CARDS.

The source cards contain the information for your Works Cited page, so it is very important to make sure you include all of the material necessary about your sources. The information is basically the same for every reference: title (the book, magazine, or other source), author or editor, place of publication, publishing company, and copyright date. If no copyright date is given, use the initials "n.d." to indicate "no date." You also need the page numbers for your parenthetical notations, but this information will be recorded on your note cards.

Additional information is needed for encyclopedias and other reference works, periodicals, and electronic sources. Because it is important to have all of the information needed for the Works Cited page, *make sure you write down everything as you do your research*. This will save you last-minute trips to the library for that date or author's name you forgot.

In addition to getting the information and recording it on your source cards, another point you might remember, especially if you use more than one library, is to record on the card which library you used for each source. This can be done by adding a small note on the bottom left of the card, making it easy to find should you need the information later.

Step 10 gives more detailed bibliographic information for the different kinds of references you need to compile the Works Cited page. Since you will need to state the information correctly on your Works Cited page, it would be a good idea to record the information on the cards as it will appear in the bibliography later.

It is also a good practice to make source cards for every reference you think you might use. If you follow this practice, you will probably have more than enough information at your fingertips and will not have to backtrack as much to find material. It is always easier to put a big X over the cards that are not useful and later discard them than it is to go back and search for more information.

As you make your source cards, a shortcut is to number your source cards in the upper right-hand corner of the card. For example, if you have ten sources, you will have cards numbered from 1 to 10. Then, as you take notes, write the number of the source in the upper right-hand corner as well. With this method you will not have to cite the complete reference; the number will indicate the location of that note. The number in the top-right corner of the note card corresponds to the source card from which you gathered the material. This method is easy to use and is a real timesaver.

The sample source cards in Figures 4.1–20 show you how to record the information needed for your Works Cited page. They are labeled to indicate which kind of source is used, and they have a number in the right-hand corner to indicate what your card will look like. The essential information is given: title of work, author(s) or editor(s), place of publication, publishing company, and copyright date. The cards have been formatted using the MLA (Modern Language Association) style.

FIGURE 4.1

Source card for a book

> 1
>
> Bagert, Brod. <u>If Only I Could Fly</u>. New Orleans:
>
>   Juliahouse. 1984.

FIGURE 4.2

Source card for an anthology

> 2
>
> Gray, Thomas. "Elegy Written in a Country
>
>   Churchyard." <u>England in Literature</u>. Eds. Helen
>
>   McDonald, John Pfordresher, and Gladys V.
>
>   Veidemanis. Glenview: Scott, Foresman, 1991.
>
>   288-89.

FIGURE 4.3

Source card for a
periodical (newspaper)

> 3
>
> Espo, David. "Gun Control Showdown Looms." <u>Advocate</u>
>
>   [Baton Rouge] 18 June 1999: 1A.

```
                                                          4
   Gray, James. "John Steinbeck." American Writers: A

        Collection of Literary Biographies. Ed. Leonard

        Unger. 4 vols. New York: Scribners, 1971.
```

FIGURE 4.4

Source card for a
reference book

```
                                                          5


   The NIV Study Bible: New International Version.

        Kenneth Barker, gen. ed. Grand Rapids:

        Zondervan, 1985.
```

FIGURE 4.5

Source card for the Bible

MLA STYLE FOR SOURCES ON THE WORLD WIDE WEB

Entries for electronic sources follow a similar format to those not on the
Web. The following list will help you determine how to use MLA style with
electronic sources. After the list, examples are given of some of the most
common kinds of Web sources. If you should still have problems, the Web
address for MLA is http://www.mla.org.

I. Name of the author, editor, compiler, or translator of the source (if available
and relevant), reversed for alphabetizing and followed by an abbreviation.

2. If no author or editor is given, begin with the title.

3. Title of poem, short story, article, or essay within a scholarly project, database, or periodical (in quotation marks); or title of a posting to a discussion list or forum (taken from the subject line and put in quotation marks), followed by the description of the "online posting."

4. Title of a book (underlined or in italics).

5. Name of the editor, compiler, or translator of the text (if revelant and if not cited earlier), preceded by the appropriate abbreviation, such as "Ed."

6. Publication information for any print version of the source.

7. Title of the scholarly project, database, periodical, or professional or personal site (underlined); or, for a professional or personal site with no title, a description such as "Home page."

8. Name of the editor of the scholarly project or database (if available).

9. Version number of the source (if not part of the title) or, for a journal, the volume number, issue number, or other identifying number.

10. Date of electronic publication, of the latest update, or of posting.

11. For a work from a subscription service, the name of the service and—if a library is the subscriber—the name and city (and state abbreviation, if necessary) of the library.

12. For a posting to a discussion list or forum, the name of the list or forum.

13. The number range or total number of pages, paragraphs, or other sections, if they are numbered.

14. Name of an institution or organization sponsoring or associated with the Web site.

15. Date when the researcher accessed the source.

16. Electronic address, or URL, of the source (in angle brackets); or, for a subscription service, the URL of the service's main page (if known) or the keyword assigned by the service.

FIGURE 4.6

Book

6

```
Dickens, Mamie. My Father as I Recall Him. Dutton,

     1987. 10 June 98

     <http://www.helsinki.fi/kasv/nokol/death.html>.
```

FIGURE 4.7

Article in a magazine

7

Kopel, David. "Arms and the Greeks." <u>Liberty</u> Aug.
1999. 4 Sept. 99
<http:www.libertysoft.com/liberty/features/
76kopel.html>.

FIGURE 4.8

Journal

8

Bower, Bruce. "Brain Images Illuminate Tourette
Syndrome." <u>Science News</u> 31 Aug. 1996. 20 June 99
<http://web3.searchbank>.

FIGURE 4.9

Poem

9

Dickinson, Emily. "I Measure Every Grief I Meet."
<u>The Poems of Emily Dickinson</u>. Ed. Thomas H.
Johnson. Belknap: 1983. <u>The Academy of
American Poets</u>. Amherst Coll. 29 Nov. 1999
<http://www.poets.org/LIT/poem/edicki06.htm>.

FIGURE 4.10

Work from a
subscription service
online

> 10
>
> Brody, Jane G. "Genetic Disorders Abstract: The New
>
>   York Times." <u>Discovering Science</u> 1 March 1995.
>
>   GaleNet. 21 June 1999.
>
>   Keyword: Tourette Syndrome.

FIGURE 4.11

Posting to a discussion
list

> 11
>
> Olson, Lilah. "Tourette Syndrome." Online posting.
>
>   3 Jan. 1998 The Babynet Discussion Forum.
>
>   29 Nov. 99
>
>   <http://www.thebabynet.com/babyboard/message/
>
>   15370.html.

FIGURE 4.12

Professional site

> 12
>
> <u>Classroom Strategies</u>. U of Texas. 14 July 1999
>
>   <http://www.eco.utex.edu/~benedict/
>
>   strategies.htm>.

13

Moon, Pretty. Home page. 14 Dec. 1999

<http://members.aol.com/_ht_a/PrttyMoon/

index.html>.

FIGURE 4.13

Personal site

14

"Facts on Tourettes Syndrome." 30 Nov. 1996. <u>NAMI</u>

(Nation's Voice on Mental Illness).

13 July 1999

<http://www.nami.org/disorder/tourette.html>.

FIGURE 4.14

Scholarly project online

15

Daniel, R. T. "The History of Western Music."

<u>Britannica Online</u>. 1995. Britannica Online:

Macropaedia. 14 June 1999

<http:/www.eb.com:180/cgi-bin/g:DocF+macro/

5004/45/0.html>.

FIGURE 4.15

Article in a reference
database

FIGURE 4.16

Article in a newspaper

16

> Reid, T. R. "Druids Return to Stonehenge."
>
> <u>Washington Post</u> 22 June 1998. 22 June 1998
>
> <http:www.washingtonpost.com/wp-srv/WPlate/
>
> 1998-06/22/045I-062298-idx.html>.

FIGURE 4.17

A nonperiodical
publication on CD-ROM

17

> Sternberg, Martin L. A. <u>The American Sign Language</u>
>
> <u>Dictionary on CD-ROM</u>. Windows vers. CD-ROM. New
>
> York: HarperCollins, 1994.

FIGURE 4.18

A television or radio
program

18

> "New Quake Concerns along the New Madrid." KOLR10
>
> Local News. CBS. 29 Nov. 1999. VHR
>
> Broadcasting. 29 Nov. 1999.

```
                                                    19
       Silberman, Steve. Interview with David Crosby.
            An Egg Thief in Cyberspace. 30 Jan. 1995.
            14 Dec. 1999
            <http://www.levity.com/digitaland/crosby95.html>.
```

FIGURE 4.19

An interview

```
                                                    20
       Veronica Kelly-Griner. "World's Freestyle Rodeo
            Championships." E-mail to Harry Kennon.
            19 Nov. 1999.
```

FIGURE 4.20

An e-mail
communication

WEB SITES

Web sites are also an area that you may want to investigate during your research, especially if you are having difficulty finding material you need. Web sites are arranged by channel and come from many different sources. Some are professional while others are personal in nature. They are accessed in the same way that you access other information from the World Wide Web—by using an address in the address box. Following are some Web sites that you may find useful with a short annotation of what they include.

1. Addictions and Life Page—a resource for those struggling with addictions of all sorts.
    <http://www.addictions.com>

2. Biography.com—a database that contains information on more than 20,000 notable people.
   <http://www.biography.com/>

3. Black Voices—a news and information area discussing music, politics, culture, and more.
   <http://www.blackvoices.com/>

4. Discovery Online—a site that features stories, contests, and conversations with experts.
   <http://www.discovery.com/>

5. Library of Congress—a site that consists of many sites containing documents, photos, movies, and sound recordings that tell America's story.
   <http://www.loc.gov/>

6. Mayo Clinic Health Oasis—a source of information on a gamut of health topics: cancer, diet, nutrition, cardiac disease, et al.
   <http://www.mayohealth.org/mayo/common/htm/index.htm>

7. Mental Health Net—a resource covering information on disorders such as depression, anxiety, panic attacks, chronic fatigue syndrome, and substance abuse.
   <http://mentalhelp.net>

8. The New York Times Book Review—the final word on literary review and commentary.
   <http://www.nytimes.com/books/home/contents.html>

9. On-Line English Grammar—a resource if you are having difficulties with the finer rules of sentence structure and parts of speech.
   <http://www.edunet.com/english/grammar>

10. WebLit—a site for information on a wide variety of authors.
    < http://is099.tsc.k12.in.us/training/curr/lang/weblit/weblit.htm >

Note: As you access these Web sites, you will notice that many of them have links that point you in other directions for research.

EXERCISE 1 ## Making Source Cards from Printed Sources

Using the correct format, make a bibliography card for the five different sources listed here. You may be able to use these sources in your research since you should have chosen a subject by now.

Number each card in the upper right-hand corner from 1 to 5, because you will be using five sources for this exercise. Be sure to record all of the information needed since it will also be used for the Works Cited page. It would be helpful, as well, to write the information in the correct form so that it will be ready to transfer to the Works Cited page when needed.

1. Book

2. Anthology (your textbook)

3. Periodical (a newspaper or magazine)

4. Reference book (specialized encyclopedia)

5. The Bible or another religious text

EXERCISE 2 ## Making Source Cards from Electronic Sources

Using the subject of your research, make bibliography cards for five electronic sources, using the correct format as shown in this Step. Number your cards 6 through 10 since you will continue numbering from Exercise 1. Record the information needed on each card since you will use that information for your Works Cited page.

6. Book

7. Article in a magazine

8. Article in a reference database

9. Work from a subscription service

10. An e-mail communication

EXERCISE 3 ## Accessing a Web Site

Choose one of the ten Web sites given on pages 59–60 and access information concerning the subject you have chosen for your research. Print at least one page of information to put in your portfolio.

5

Taking Notes and Recording Them on Note Cards

In addition to source cards, other kinds of cards that you will use in preparing your research paper are quotation cards, summary cards, and, possibly, paraphrase cards. Some instructors also suggest another kind of card which could prove to be quite valuable—the *idea card* on which you record ideas you have come up with in your research and that you might want to develop as you go along. We will discuss and give examples for each of these.

MAKING QUOTATION CARDS

Quotation cards are those on which you record material exactly as it was taken from the source. This means that *anything* that is copied should have quotation marks around it because it is a direct quote. Students sometimes think that if the material is not an exact statement a person made, such as in dialog, then it does not need quotation marks around it. This is not true. Anything that is quoted directly from the source must be enclosed within quotation marks.

It is also very important that you record the information exactly as written. If a word is misspelled in the quote, write the word *sic* (meaning "thus") in square brackets [ ] immediately after the word so your instructor will know that it is not your error. In that way you make it clear that you have quoted the material exactly as it was written.

The quotation card shown in Figure 5.1 illustrates how important it is to record exact information. As shown, the number in the upper right-hand corner refers to the source from which the material was gathered. In this case the source was *Children with Tourette Syndrome: A Parents' Guide.* (See Figure 4.1.) The page number is noted in the upper left-hand corner, an easy way to keep track of where the quoted material was found. Remember that information will need to be referenced in the paper. In addition, *each card is given a title*, even though the material may have come from the same source, because you should have only one idea or one quote on the card pertaining to that title. If you need to continue the material to another card, simply alphabetize the next cards. Use l-b and so on for the succeeding cards entitled "Teasing a TS Child" from the same source. Organizing the cards in this way will help immensely when the time comes to sort them out and write the outline.

---

p. 194   Teasing a TS Child   1

"Adults both at home and at school must make a con-
certed effort to prevent your child from being
teased by other children. Teasing is tolerated far
too often in the schools and is devastating to a
child's self-esteem. When teasing occurs, it is not
your child's fault. Rather it results from the
inability of teachers and other adults to control
the behavior of other children. Teachers and princi-
pals must explain to other children that TS symptoms
are not under your child's control, and that teasing
will not be tolerated in school."

FIGURE 5.1

Sample quotation card

If you use this material in your paper, you will use a form of referencing called parenthetical notation, which is used by the *MLA* (Modern Language Association) *Handbook for Writers of Research Papers*. Simply stated, the term *parenthetical notation* means that the writer will include the page numbers and/or the author in parentheses after the citation. If you introduce the quotation by giving the author's name, only the page numbers of the material cited are included in the parentheses at the end of the quote. However, if you do not introduce the quotation with the author's name, you will put his or her name in parentheses along with the page number at the end of the reference. Keep in mind that the page number is very important to include along with the author's name, since that points the reader to the exact place you found your material. Either method works well as long as it blends into the paper. More information is given about parenthetical notation in the referencing section starting on page 89.

Making Summary Cards

Summary cards contain what the name implies—summaries or shortened versions of the material. The information on the summary card contains the main points of the particular research in a nutshell. Summaries are helpful because they are the nucleus of your thinking. One librarian suggests that students close their books and then write a summary of what they have just read. In that way, she says, they retain the important material without the clutter of irrelevant material. You might try this to help you visualize the most important information in an article or a chapter in a book. As you write the summary, you will begin to form the habit of discarding what you do not need and better retaining what you do need. This will be of great help to you in your research.

When you summarize, you do not have to put quotation marks around the summary, but you do need to give credit to the source in your references. If you use key words or ideas within the summary, however, they should be enclosed with quotation marks because they are not yours. They belong to the author, and you must give him or her credit. The summary card shown in Figure 5.2, using the same information as the quotation card in Figure 5.1, demonstrates how to summarize.

FIGURE 5.2

Sample summary card

```
p. 194             Teasing a TS Child              1


The TS child is often teased at school unnecessarily

because teachers do not make the effort to control

children who do the teasing. This often causes the

TS child to lose self-esteem. This can be remedied

if the adults in charge make it clear that teasing

will not be tolerated.
```

As you can see from the card, the essential information from the quotation card is there, but it is said in a shortened form in the researcher's own words. In introducing this quotation, you might begin by saying something like this:

```
According to Haerle, the child with TS is often teased

at school, which makes him even more likely to lose

self-esteem. This could be remedied if teachers would

make the effort to control children who do the teasing

and if they make it clear that teasing will not be

tolerated (194).
```

By introducing the summary in this way, you are giving credit to the person who wrote the article. Because the selection is summarized, however, quotation marks are not needed. As with this example, you may even rewrite your summary card to blend better with the introduction. The parenthetical notation after the summary indicates where it came from, but there is no need to record the author's name because it was given earlier.

MAKING PARAPHRASE CARDS

Paraphrase cards are another kind of summary card, but they are different in that they paraphrase the work of the writer. These cards are often more beneficial than a true summary of the work. With both kinds of summaries, the material is put in your own words rather than your simply quoting the words of the writer.

Sometimes you may think you are summarizing a passage when you are actually paraphrasing the passage. There is nothing wrong with paraphrasing material, but you should know how to paraphrase. If you do not, you will soon begin to plagiarize, and that is a serious offense. To *plagiarize* means to take the writings of another person and to use them as your own, whereas to *paraphrase* means to state the meaning of the passage in other words. This means that you retain the idea of the writer, but you state it in your own words. A paraphrase is usually about the same length as the original, or it could possibly be even longer than the original. It often follows the original line for line. The difference in a paraphrase and quoting from the author is that you have used your words rather than the author's. That is very important to remember in writing a paraphrase card. Otherwise you lapse into the habit of combining the author's words with yours rather than making them totally your own.

The sample card in Figure 5.3 shows a paraphrase of the material quoted in Figure 5.1 and summarized in Figure 5.2. The paraphrase follows the original quotation almost line for line, using the researcher's own words yet retaining the sense of the passage and the style of the writer.

FIGURE 5.3

Sample paraphrase card

```
p. 194            Teasing a TS Child            1


Parents and other adults at home and at school need

to do everything they can to see that the child with

Tourette is not teased. Teasing is a form of abuse

that hinders the child's development and causes him

or her to lose self-esteem. It's important that the

child understands that when others tease him or her,

the fault lies not within himself or herself as much

as with teachers and other adults who fail to keep

other children from bothering him or her. Therefore,

it is absolutely necessary that the people in

authority inform other children that TS symptoms are

not voluntary and that teasing will be prohibited in

the school.
```

When putting the paraphrased material in your paper, though, do as you did with the summary card: Give credit to the writer. Either introduce the paraphrase with his or her name and put the page number in parentheses at the end, or put both his or her name and the page number in the parentheses at the end. Because you used the writer's ideas and form of writing, credit is due to him or her. The author of the material is protected by intellectual property rights; thus, when you use his or her material without proper documentation, you are plagiarizing. Simply by giving the proper notation, you avoid plagiarizing or stealing the writer's work.

As you can see from this example, the paraphrase runs line for line with the original, but it does not use the same words that the author used. In the paper, though, credit will be given to the writer.

Making Idea Cards

Idea cards are not absolutely necessary; however, they do serve a purpose. As you read the material for your research, you will likely come upon an idea that you don't want to forget. In order to keep the idea intact, the best thing to do is jot down those ideas. You can reference them similar to the way you reference other cards. Put a number on the right top corner of the card to indicate where the idea was from and then put a phrase or so in the title part of the card to indicate what the idea is about. With an idea card, it isn't necessary to use correct grammar or punctuation since it is simply something you don't want to forget and might want to follow up on later. With the idea written down, you will have the option of following up on it or not.

Understanding Plagiarism

As mentioned earlier, students sometimes plagiarize in their papers, often without meaning to do so. Lack of intent, however, does not excuse those who plagiarize. In recent years a politician who was running for a high public office had to step down because someone discovered he had plagiarized in a college research paper, even though it happened more than twenty years before. To say it was done inadvertently did not carry much weight; it was still considered dishonest. Another case in recent years involved a Harvard professor who resigned for the same reason, and in still another case much publicity was given to a pre-law student who failed to properly attribute a source she used in her research paper. She had not put quotation marks around the material but had referred to the passage in her footnotes. Princeton denied her diploma because she had, in effect, said the material was a paraphrase or were her own words by leaving off the quotation marks. Law schools to which she had applied were also notified.

Plagiarism is immoral; it is the same thing as stealing from another person because you are stealing that person's words. On college campuses, plagiarism is called *premeditated dishonesty*, and the penalty is more severe than cheating on a test. While each university has its own rules, in most universities this offense means permanent expulsion. No matter how ethical or honest you become later, you would still be denied access to that particular university. Plagiarism is not condoned by anyone; it is a serious offense.

Following is an example taken from *The Unwelcome Companion: An Insider's View of Tourette Syndrome* giving correct attribution to the source. Following it is an example of plagiarism of the same source. Perhaps by reading both samples you will see what is meant by plagiarism.

Correctly Quoting Material

In the fly of his book, *The Unwelcome Companion*, Rick Fowler aptly describes what it is like to have Tourette Syndrome:

```
When I breathe, it breathes. When I speak, it speaks.
When I try to sleep, it won't let me. Whatever I attempt
to do, it's there—waiting to spoil the moment. To a doc-
tor, it's a disorder, a medical oddity. To an onlooker,
it's a spectacle—perhaps humorous, perhaps grotesque. To
me, it's a monster, a demon, a hellish beast who has no
right to exist in my world or anyone else's. It's my
unwelcome companion.
```

You may have noticed that there were no quotation marks around the long quotation (of more than four lines). The indentation shows that it is a quotation and therefore no quotation marks are needed. The introduction to the quote also states the author's name, which makes it unnecessary to give the author's name within parentheses at the end. Since the quotation was by itself on a page with no numbering, no page number was given in parentheses.

Incorrectly Quoting Material, or Plagiarizing

```
Tourette takes such a hold on the person that he feels
suffocated. When he inhales, it inhales; when he opens
his mouth to talk, it opens its mouth. In everything he
does, it is there to make havoc of the moment. Those in
the medical field call it an anomaly, but those who
watch the person with Tourette think it is an interest-
ing sight. The person who has Tourette may feel so con-
sumed with it that he feels another person is living
inside him, one he had rather not be there.
```

This example clearly illustrates that the writer is using the same material, changed only slightly. Many of the same words or images are used. The writer has paraphrased Fowler's description of the way he feels. It would have been legitimate to record the material in this manner if a reference were given to Fowler. But if the writer does not give credit to Fowler, he or she is simply plagiarizing, taking credit that belongs to the author.

The rules for avoiding plagiarism are easy to follow, but if they are not used, you can get into a lot of trouble. It is to your advantage to learn the rules and abide by them. Then you do not have to worry about committing the crime of stealing another person's words.

The following rules are listed to make it easier for you to know how to avoid plagiarizing and thus risk the consequences of literary or intellectual property theft.

Avoiding Plagiarism

The following guidelines can help you avoid plagiarism:

1. *Always* put quotation marks around any direct statement from someone else's work.
2. Give credit to the author for any *paraphrase* of his or her ideas or statements, even though quotation marks are not used, because these ideas are clearly not your own.
3. Reference any material, ideas, or thoughts you found in a specific source if it is evident that they came from your reading and are not common knowledge.
4. Do not reference material that is *common knowledge*. This refers to biographical material such as birthplace, date of birth, death, and other general knowledge that people know without having to look up the information. For example, the statement, "Skin cancer is caused by too much exposure to the rays of the sun and may not be noticed for years," is information that is common knowledge.
5. Reference any summary—even if it is your own words—of a discussion from one of your sources.
6. Reference any charts, graphs, or tables that are created by others or that you make with someone else's information. Put the reference immediately below the title of the chart, graph, or table.

Though a detailed discussion of plagiarism may seem irrelevant at this point, it is very significant. If you start writing your note cards using correct references and quotations, you will not need to worry about what is a quotation and what is a summary when you begin writing your paper.

Note cards are a must, even in the computer age when photocopiers and other duplicating machines are available. It is much more time-consuming to have to thumb through reams of material to know what is usable than to use note cards taken from the photocopied material.

If you have a computer, however, you may prefer to take notes on the computer instead of using note cards. This is called a *note sheet*, and it is more easily read if you double-space your notes. Follow the identical rules for quotation cards and summary cards. That means you put the same information on the sheet as you would on a note card: source number in the top right-hand corner, page number in the top left-hand corner, and subject of the card centered at the top of the page. Only one subject should be included on a note sheet.

Whether you use note cards or note sheets, take as many notes as possible. The more notes you have, the greater potential you have to produce a better paper. After all, research is about selecting and eliminating useful and useless information—the more you have, the more complete your research.

EXERCISE 1   Quotation Card
_____

By now you have some idea of the subject for your research. For this exercise, choose a source that you used in Step 4, Exercise I. Make a quotation card from the source following the direction given in this step. Give the card a number in the right-hand corner, a page number in the left-hand corner, and a title for the information on the card.

EXERCISE 2   Summary Card
_____

Using the same quotation from Exercise 1, write a summary in your own words on a note card. Reference the material correctly.

EXERCISE 3   Paraphrase Card
_____

Using the material from Exercise 1, write a paraphrase on a note card. Reference the material correctly. Compare your paraphrase to the original to see whether you have put the material in your own words line by line or whether you have used ideas and keywords from the author. For purposes of instructor critiquing, include a copy of the original text with Exercises 1, 2, and 3.

Forming a Thesis

By now you have read enough material to arrive at some direction for writing your paper. You have narrowed your subject down to a workable topic, so the next step is to write a *thesis,* or an objective, for your paper. This means that you will present an idea—your thesis—that you will defend through your writing. Everything in your paper will support the thesis, which you will argue from your point of view. While it is recognized that some research papers are, for the most part, factual or informative, all of them are persuasive to the degree that in your research, you will prove your assertion, or thesis.

ARRIVING AT A THESIS

There are several points to consider in arriving at a thesis. First, you must decide on which approach to take now that you know something about your subject. One way to determine your approach is to brainstorm ideas that you have gathered through your research. Jot them all down, then cross out the unsuitable ideas until you arrive at one you can support with your research. For example, in determining what would be a good thesis for a paper on Tourette Syndrome, Ellen brainstormed the following ideas:

(1) Tourette Syndrome affects more boys than girls, and its causes and resulting effects are controversial, making it difficult for the child with Tourette to be accepted by society.

(2) Tourette Syndrome is an illness that continues to be misunderstood scientifically and at the same time is even more misunderstood by society, which causes the person with Tourette to suffer untold agony as well as those around him or her to be affected.

(3) Understanding Tourette Syndrome as an illness is the first step in understanding the person who has Tourette, thus helping those around the individual to adapt to the illness and the person more appropriately.

(4) While there is debate about what causes Tourette Syndrome, the fact is that the person with Tourette faces almost insurmountable obstacles because of the ignorance of society and the resulting reaction to his or her actions.

(5) The person with Tourette Syndrome lives in a world to himself, often feeling isolated from others because of their reaction to him and because of his own feelings of being different.

(6) Schools and society as a whole are doing very little to recognize the problem of Tourette Syndrome and to help the person with Tourette feel accepted as a part of society.

As you can see, each of the statements can evolve into a thesis statement for a paper on Tourette Syndrome. Each statement also carries with it the idea that the child is not the only person who suffers; others around him or her also must learn how to cope. It will be up to the writer to determine which point will be more effective in her research paper.

Another way to help you arrive at a thesis is to ask the same questions you used in narrowing your topic: *who, what, when, where, why,* and *how.* These questions can be asked with different types of papers, for by exploring them you will be able to home in on your thesis. For example, if you plan to use an analytical approach in your paper, you will be more concerned with the *what* and the *how* of your subject, and your thesis will reflect that stance. If you choose to develop your paper by explanation, you will concern your-self more with *who, what, when, where,* and perhaps *why.* If you are clearly writing an argumentative paper, you will think more about *why* and *how* and perhaps *who* or *what.* As you ask these questions, you will develop an objective for your paper that you can state in one sentence—your thesis.

There are no hard-and-fast rules about how to choose a thesis. Brainstorming ideas or asking the questions *who, what, when, where, why,* and *how* and looking over the material you have researched can help you decide what you want to defend in your paper. There are, however, some other points to consider in determining whether you have a viable thesis—one that will work well with your subject. And even though some papers do not lend themselves well to argument, the thesis must be a statement that can be supported in order to ascertain whether the purpose of the paper has been carried out. Otherwise, as your instructor reads your paper, he or she will not be able to determine if you have adequately supported anything! There will be little direction to your paper.

Developing a Sound Thesis

The following guidelines can help you to develop a good thesis:

1. A thesis should be one arguable point. While writing an informative paper may not lend itself as well to argument as an argumentative paper, your thesis is arguable to the point that you are presenting your point of view. Another person could write on the same subject and approach it entirely differently. Because your point is debatable to whatever extent, your approach to the subject is what you will support in your research paper. Your research is simply gathering material others have compiled to support the point of view you have chosen for your paper.

2. A thesis should not be a question. If your thesis asks a question, the reader has no idea what you are trying to support and what stance you are taking. Because of that, it will be a statement, not a question.

3. The thesis should be restricted, which means that it should cover only those points you intend to discuss, thereby providing a nutshell of your paper in one sentence.

4. The thesis should have unity. This means that it will have a single purpose, not a double purpose or two different ideas in your paper. Sometimes this purpose is called a single principle by which the paper is constructed. Even with a comparison or a comparison and contrast paper, there should still be one overall purpose, or thesis, that unites the two areas you are investigating.

Refining Your Thesis

One of the most difficult parts of writing the research paper is finalizing your thesis statement. The reason for that is exactly what you have just read about in developing a sound thesis statement. You are aware of the fact that it is the nucleus of your paper and you must include the main idea of what you want to incorporate in your paper. For that reason, you will spend some time making sure that it is a good thesis statement.

It is very unlikely that your first thesis will be the one you will choose for your paper. Your attitude toward your subject may change slightly as you write, necessitating a change in your thesis. This means that you are refining your thesis, cutting out parts that you cannot support and adding others that you can support. Of course, some truly experienced writers are adept enough to have an implied thesis, but if you follow this route, everything in your paper will support the implication because of its being evident.

Earlier, you looked at some possible thesis statements concerning the paper on Tourette Syndrome. Because there are so many angles from which this subject might be approached, Ellen understood that she must be careful to choose exactly what will be reflected in her research. After reading from a number of sources, she found it difficult to get away from the idea that, while the scientific field has made strides in diagnosing Tourette Syndrome, it is still often misdiagnosed. She found that the person who has Tourette Syndrome not only suffers from the illness, but others around the person also suffer. Therefore, she chose the second thesis statement as her preliminary thesis statement and will develop her paper by cause and effect.

Follow Ellen as she develops the thesis that she will use and note her decisions about what to include or not include. Keep in mind that Ellen has already decided that her research is aimed toward a misdiagnosis of Tourette and a lack of acceptance of the person who has Tourette and the ensuing problems of not being accepted.

Poor Thesis

Tourette Syndrome is an illness that continues to be misunderstood scientifically and at the same time is even more misunderstood by society, which causes the person with Tourette to suffer untold agony as well as those around him or her to be affected.

First of all, note that the thesis does not include the idea of Tourette Syndrome's being misdiagnosed, which she wanted to include. Also, at least three other things are questionable in the statement:

1. It "continues to be misunderstood scientifically"—This statement indicates there were preceding statements leading to its being misunderstood before. If Ellen chooses to use this, she will have to be sure to include this misunderstanding scientifically as an earlier part of her introduction so that it will blend in with the thesis.

2. It is "even more misunderstood by society"—What does she mean? How will she show it is "even more misunderstood" in her paper? Is Tourette more misunderstood by "all" society?

3. "The person with Tourette will suffer untold agony"—This part also demands some qualification. How will Ellen show the "untold" agony? Do "all" Tourette sufferers experience this?

You can see that Ellen is making some rather broad generalizations. In addition to the qualifiers, the thesis itself needs to be tightened up so that it will not be too wordy. Now, look at how Ellen restated the thesis so that it states more of what she wants to include.

Better Thesis

The misunderstanding of Tourette Syndrome by physicians and psychologists and their misdiagnosis of the disorder along with the lack of knowledge of Tourette by the general public often causes problems for the individual with Tourette as well as for those associated with him or her.

This thesis statement is improved. The qualifying statements have been toned down, but it still needs some tightening up grammatically.

Finally, look at the third thesis statement that Ellen chose for her paper. As you can see, it incorporates the idea that Tourette Syndrome is misdiagnosed and misunderstood and that the child is affected as well as those around him or her.

Best Thesis

The misunderstanding and misdiagnosis of Tourette Syndrome by physicians and psychologists, along with a lack of knowledge by the general public, often causes problems for the individual with Tourette as well as for those associated with him or her.

It is clear from this statement what the paper will encompass. It will emphasize two points: (1) that Tourette is an illness misunderstood and misdiagnosed scientifically—by physicians and psychologists—and misunderstood by the general public and (2) because of this, the person who has Tourette is affected as well as those associated with him or her. Even though two points are in the thesis, they are connected by cause and effect. Each part blends into and supports the other. It is easy to see, too, that Ellen's thesis expresses an opinion; it is not a question; it is restricted to the areas to be covered in the paper; and it is unified.

As you write your paper, you will want to follow the same procedure Ellen used to develop a thesis statement that she could support in her paper. You will likely go from a poor thesis statement to a better one and finally to one that is more concise and more unified.

DEFENDING YOUR THESIS

Now that the thesis for your paper has been formed, you need to think about the opposite point of view. Any well-written thesis, because it is debatable to some extent, should have an opposing point of view—called an *antithesis*. By looking at the opposite side, you can determine if your thesis has merit, if it can truly be defended, and if someone can present an opposing argument. The hallmark of a good argument is that you are able to defend it, which means knowing what the opposition might counter in an antithesis.

In determining possible antitheses using the Tourette Syndrome example, Ellen pondered the following questions:

(1) Why is Tourette Syndrome misunderstood scientifically?
(2) Is Tourette Syndrome misunderstood by all in the medical field or is it just misunderstood by some?
(3) What evidence exists of the medical community's misunderstanding of Tourette Syndrome?
(4) How does society show a misunderstanding of Tourette Syndrome?
(5) How does the person suffer greatly?
(6) How do those around the individual also suffer?

As she looked at possible answers to the questions, she realized that others might question her supposition regarding Tourette. Because she realized what her opposition might be, this only strengthened her resolve to provide good support for her thesis. Ellen's antithesis looked like this:

While it may be true that some in the scientific field do not understand Tourette Syndrome and may possibly misdiagnose it, it would seem far-fetched to think that all of society misunderstands Tourette Syndrome, thus causing problems for the sufferer and those around him or her.

The point of Ellen's antithesis was to question whether the research can support such assertions as the thesis proposed regarding the scientific field and whether there is adequate support for the statement of misunderstanding regarding Tourette Syndrome. Her antithesis also questioned the suffering of the individual and those around him or her caused by this misunderstanding.

As you have thought of questions concerning the opposition to your thesis, you should be able to formulate an antithesis or opposite point of view. You should also see that your thesis is made stronger by knowing others may take opposition to it. It is not necessary, however, to include the actual words of the antithesis in your paper. Instead, you may refer to it in different words or change it to suit your writing needs. If you do decide to use the antithesis in your paper, it would follow in the paragraph after the introduction. More discussion of the placement and merging of the opposing point of view is given in Step 9, Writing the First Draft.

WRITING A THESIS FOR A LITERARY PAPER

Writing a thesis for a literary paper is somewhat different from writing one for a nonliterary subject, and yet the rules for developing a sound thesis are the same. The biggest difference involves your having read the work first in order to understand it and to know which angle to develop your research from. After reading the work and deciding on your approach, you then develop some possible thesis statements. For example, suppose you chose *The Return of the Native*, one of Thomas Hardy's books. Some possible thesis statements might be the following:

1. In *The Return of the Native,* Thomas Hardy shows that nature or fate, represented by Egdon Heath, is superior to human nature represented by Eustacia Vye, proving that man is not master of his fate.
2. While fate seems to be an imposing force, the characters' motivations, decisions, and actions cause their own tragic ends.
3. The characters in *The Return of the Native* represent the human race with their deaths symbolic of their lives, showing triumph as well as defeat.
4. Thomas Hardy was a social reformer as shown in his indictment of the society of his day in *The Return of the Native* as well as in his other Wessex novels.
5. Thomas Hardy's pessimism and loss of religious faith are shown in his treatment of superstition and his attitude toward religion in *The Return of the Native.*

While these are only suggestions for possible thesis statements, you can see that there is no way to research these topics without having first read the book, *The Return of the Native*. After you have determined a tentative thesis, you can then, as suggested with the Tourette paper, decide on possible opposing points.

For example, suppose you choose the fifth thesis statement, "Thomas Hardy's pessimism and loss of religious faith are shown in his treatment of superstition and his attitude toward religion in *The Return of the Native*."

Some questions to consider might be the following:

1. What are some ways that Hardy used superstition?
2. How did he view religion in a negative way?
3. How did superstition affect the novel adversely?
4. If Hardy has Clym Yeobright become a preacher in the end, how does that show his loss of faith?

From these questions, an antithesis might be that Thomas Hardy's portrayal of superstition and religion were more a matter of beliefs in the nineteenth century than his loss of faith. You can see, then, that the writer will need to work hard to prove that his or her thesis is stronger than the antithesis. He or she will use examples from the book, research what others have said, and look at the times in which Thomas Hardy lived in order to support the thesis effectively.

Now that you have a thesis and an antithesis for your paper, whether it is a literary paper or a nonliterary paper, you also have a plan of support as well as how it may be countered. The next thing to do is organize your paper. The note cards you have written will help you organize your subject. If you stack all of the note cards with one subject in one pile and then do the same for other subjects, you can see the form your paper will take automatically. A definite pattern will probably emerge because you have more material on some subjects than you do on others. This helps you determine the major and minor points of your paper. You may also realize that you need to do more research on certain parts. Having to do further research is often necessary and can be seen more clearly in an outline of your paper.

Writing an outline is the next step in writing your paper. An outline will help you keep on track and be better organized. It shows you the major and minor points of your paper, and it also shows whether you are needlessly emphasizing some parts because you found more material in those areas. In addition, an outline can help you think logically, showing that certain points naturally come before others and some points are less important than others.

The standard outline format in Step 7 is used by schools and colleges alike. The example shown is the outline of the paper on Tourette Syndrome. Now that you are familiar with this paper topic, you can see how it emerges through the outline.

EXERCISE 1   Forming a Thesis

Look at the quotation you copied for your practice note cards in Step 5 and, even though you have not yet done much in-depth research, formulate a possible thesis. Remember the criteria for a thesis as you work.

1. Brainstorm any ideas you can think of concerning your thesis and jot them down.

2. Write out questions that might help you form a thesis, beginning with *who, what, when, where, why,* and *how.*

3. Use your imagination and write a possible thesis for the subject you have chosen, remembering that it will likely change as your paper develops.

EXERCISE 2   Changing a Poor Thesis Statement into a Better One

Read the following poor thesis statement, then see how it progresses into a better thesis statement:

Poor Statement: Children who are neglected in the home become targets for abuse.

Better Statement: Children who are neglected in the home are open to abuse and rarely rise above their home life.

Best Statement: Children who are neglected in the home are vulnerable to abuse and thus develop low self-esteem, which causes them to have little ambition.

As you can see from the final thesis statement, the major point to develop is the neglect in the home, which then triggers abuse, low self-esteem, and lack of ambition.

Now, do the same for the thesis statement you did in Exercise 1.

Poor Statement:

Better Statement:

Best Statement:

EXERCISE 3   Checking the Validity of Your Thesis

From the thesis you formed in Exercise 1, determine the validity of your thesis by checking it against the following questions. Refer to "Developing a Sound Thesis" on page 73.

1. Does your thesis have one major point to defend that you think will be adequate for the research you plan?

2. Does your thesis cover only the points you think you will discuss or do parts of it stray from the single principle?

3. Does the thesis reflect your thinking even though your paper may be mostly informative rather than persuasive?

4. If your thesis is an implied thesis, how have you stated it so that the reader will understand what your research will be about?

5. Share your thesis with a partner and have him or her evaluate it according to these questions.

EXERCISE 4   Forming an Antithesis

Develop an antithesis, or opposite point of view, to the thesis you wrote in Exercise 1. Write a paragraph, which could be used in your paper, with the opposing points of your antithesis. Keep this in your portfolio for future reference.

Making an Outline

The outline you prepare will be the guiding force for your paper. You have gathered your material, you have considered it carefully, and you have written your thesis. Now you are ready to put everything in order.

First, write down the purpose for your research, which is designed to prove your thesis. The following phrases are often used: *to compare, to prove, to analyze, to create, to determine, to examine, to explore, to show, to describe,* or *to record.*

Ellen's purpose for her paper on Tourette Syndrome follows:

    Purpose: To explore why Tourette Syndrome continues
    to be misunderstood by the medical field as well as
    by the general public, thus causing problems for
    the individual affected as well as those who are
    associated with the person.

SELECTING SUBJECT HEADINGS

After you have written the purpose, look back over your note cards and organize them according to the subject headings on each card. You might find your paper taking on a different slant after you have organized them. As you can see from the sample outline on pages 84–85, there was a stack of cards entitled "Definition of Tourette Syndrome." Along with that stack, there was an accompanying stack of note sheets (from computer research) and note cards entitled "Misdiagnosing Tourette Syndrome." At the outset of the research, it was evident that many in the medical field have difficulty defining exactly what Tourette is and therefore misdiagnose the illness.

Other stacks of cards were labeled "Lack of Acceptance of Tourette," "Living with Tourette," "Society's Reaction to Tourette," "Personal Stories—People with Tourette," and a stack entitled "Causes of Tourette." The stack entitled "Lack of Acceptance of Tourette" was so large that it was subdivided into other stacks, some dealing with negative effects, some with positive effects. Because these cards are reflections of research aimed toward supporting the thesis, the researcher divided the cards into the major points of the thesis: misdiagnosing by the medical field, society's lack of knowledge and acceptance of Tourette, and problems the child who has Tourette encounters. From these major divisions, she then sorted the cards into other stacks that would become minor points or subheadings in the outline— points dealing with the individual who has the illness and other points dealing with the person's parents, siblings, and other family members.

Just as you can see the scope of the paper on Tourette and how it fits into outline form, you should be able to do the same with your paper. First, sort your cards out according to your thesis and then work from there to form your outline.

The outline is divided into Roman numeral divisions that are the major points and then subdivided into smaller divisions that become the other supporting points. The introduction and conclusion are not subdivided, even though they may or may not be included as major points in the outline. The sample topic outline shows the introduction and conclusion as part of the outline, whereas the sentence outline omits them. Either way is permissible; however, if you include the introduction in the outline, the conclusion must also be included.

FOLLOWING CORRECT OUTLINE FORM

The correct form for outlines is straightforward. The first level is the Roman numeral "I," which must be followed by Roman numeral "II" and other Roman numerals if needed. The next division is a capital letter "A" followed by "B" with other letters if needed. The Arabic numeral "1" comes next, followed by a "2." If you subdivide into smaller units, the lowercase letter "a" comes next followed by a lowercase letter "b." Each level may also have further subdivisions. An important point to remember about outlines, however, is that *just one point cannot stand alone*. For example, if you have an A, you must have a B; if you have an arabic numeral 1, you must have a 2, and so forth. The reason for this is that if a point cannot be divided into at least two parts, then it should not be divided at all. The heading will give the information needed.

The form of an outline may be a sentence outline or a topic outline. Whichever form your instructor chooses demands consistency, which means that you must use the form throughout the outline. In other words, you cannot start writing in sentences and then decide to use phrases or topics and then revert to sentences again. The points must be kept in the same form throughout. You should also use parallel structure in stating your points. This means that you will use the same type of phrases or topics with each heading or subheading. However, your phrasing within each Roman numeral heading does not have to be the same with each subheading. The sample outline of the paper on Tourette Syndrome shows how this works.

Sometimes you may find it helpful to construct a working outline before your formal outline. A working outline is what its name implies—one that you are working from as you write your paper, not necessarily what you will end up with in your final outline. A working outline helps you know what you have to work with and what needs to be added to or discarded. For the most part, you would include only the major points of the outline, which could be changed as needed. For example, Ellen used the following working outline for her paper on Tourette Syndrome:

A. Definition of Tourette Syndrome
B. Diagnosing Tourette Syndrome
C. Misdiagnosing Tourette Syndrome
D. Causes of Tourette
E. Misunderstanding of Tourette Syndrome
F. Problems People Face Who Have Tourettes
G. Effects of Tourette Syndrome on Family

In addition to a working outline's being beneficial to you as you write, your instructor may want to see a working outline before you begin your paper. This will help him or her see if you are on the right track or if you are putting too much emphasis on points that are not a part of the thesis. In addition, your instructor may ask you to turn in a final typed outline with your paper. In the final outline, your major points will be the topic sentences within the paper or will be references to the topic sentences, such as with a topic outline. He or she may want to refer to the outline while grading your paper to see if you are doing what your outline proposes.

As pointed out earlier, depending upon your instructor's instructions, you may have a choice concerning whether to include the introduction and conclusion as a part of the outline. If you do include these as points, remember they *cannot* be subdivided. They will stand alone, as shown in the topic outline of the Tourette Syndrome paper.

Some instructors also like to see the thesis included as a part of the outline. If so, it should come immediately after the title of the paper. The topic outline that follows shows how this can be done. Keeping the thesis in front of you as you form your outline helps you to see if you are following the points made in your thesis. You will note, as suggested in Step 6, that the thesis has changed slightly from the proposed thesis. The change was necessary to fit better with the introduction.

Topic Outline

Tourette Syndrome: A Misunderstood Problem

Thesis: Misdiagnosis of Tourette Syndrome by physicians or psychologists and the lack of information of Tourette by the general public cause problems for the individual with Tourette as well as for those associated with the person.

    I.   Introduction
   II.   Definition of Tourette Syndrome
  III.   Misdiagnosing Tourette Syndrome in medical fields
         A. Symptoms: not based on diagnostic test
         B. Clinical: based on history and exam
   IV.   Causes of Tourette
         A. Neurological
         B. Inherited
         C. Neurochemical Malfunction
    V.   The general public's lack of knowledge of Tourette
         A. Of what Tourette is
         B. Of causes of Tourette
         C. Of symptoms associated with Tourette
             1. Ostracized as result of Tourette
             2. Regarded as demon possessed
         D. Of effects of Tourette Syndrome

    VI. Lack of acceptance of Tourette in business world

         A. Rigid concept of professional poise

         B. Respect greater benefit than being liked

   VII. Lack of acceptance in school among peers

         A. Negative effects

              1. Ryan Farrell

              2. Dr. Larry Burd

              3. Joshua P. Karch

              4. Ten-year-old Mark

         B. Positive effects

              1. More forgiving

              2. More understanding

              3. More accepting

  VIII. Effect of Tourette on Family

         A. Parents

         B. Siblings

              1. Nick Farrell

              2. Julie Hughes

    IX. Conclusion

Sentence Outline

(*Note:* This outline does not include introduction or conclusion.)

       Tourette Syndrome: A Misunderstood Problem

Thesis: Misdiagnosis of Tourette Syndrome by physicians or psychologists and the lack of information of Tourette by the general public cause problems for the individual with Tourette as well as for those associated with the person.

     I. Tourette was first described by Gilles de la Tourette in 1885.

II. Tourette is often misdiagnosed in the medical fields.

    A. Some diagnose Tourette on the basis of symptoms, not diagnostic test.

    B. Others diagnose Tourette clinically and by test.

III. The causes of Tourette are known now.

    A. Tourette is a neurological disorder and not a mental deficiency.

    B. Tourette is inherited by dominant genes from both parents.

    C. Tourette is caused by a neurochemical malfunction.

IV. Tourette is still misunderstood by the general public.

    A. They do not know what Tourette is.

    B. They do not understand the causes of Tourette.

    C. They do not understand the symptoms of Tourette.

        1. The child is often ostracized as a result of Tourette.

        2. The child is regarded as demon possessed by some.

    D. They do not understand the effects of Tourette.

V. Tourette is not accepted in the business world.

    A. The business world has a rigid concept of professional poise.

    B. The business world regards respect as a greater benefit than being liked.

VI. The Tourette child is often not accepted in school among peers.

    A. Children make fun of the person with Tourette, causing negative effects.

        1. Ryan Farrell describes how children call him names.

        2. Dr. Larry Burd describes how children often feel isolated.

       3.   Joshua P. Karch gives accounts of kids being made fun of.

       4.   Ten-year-old Mark recalls kids calling him weird.

   B.   Positive effects do happen in spite of negative effects.

       1.   Sometimes the child is more forgiving because he learns how to forgive through having Tourette.

       2.   Sometimes the child shows more understanding because he can relate to other people's problems.

       3.   Sometimes the child becomes more accepting of others because he knows what it is like to be teased.

VII.   Tourette Syndrome also affects the family.

   A.   Parents are affected because of ridicule and lack of understanding.

   B.   Siblings are affected as well as parents.

       1.   Nick Farrell describes what it is like to have a brother with TS.

       2.   Julie Hughes reacts positively to her brother with TS.

Most instructors prefer the topic outline over the sentence outline simply because the sentence outline tends to be made after the paper has been written; thus the outline serves no real purpose. On the other hand, a well-written outline can be the guiding force of your paper because it keeps you on track and helps you to determine if your research is adequate and useful.

EXERCISE 1   Working Outline

By now you have done some research; you have bibliography cards, note cards or note sheets, and you have a tentative thesis. Sort your cards according to subjects and make a working outline for your paper. Submit your working outline to your instructor for review.

EXERCISE 2   Topic Outline

After your working outline has been returned to you, make a topic outline for your paper. Include your thesis as well. Keep both of these exercises in your portfolio.

8

Adding References to Your Paper

Adding references to your paper is not difficult once you understand the process. You already have the information in your note cards and source or bibliography cards. Inserting the references is usually a matter of transferring the material and giving credit to the proper source.

Again, it is important to emphasize the necessity of not plagiarizing. Step 5 gave rules for avoiding plagiarism. Simply stated, this means giving credit to the author for material or ideas rather than accepting credit as your own. This is done using parenthetical notations immediately following the usage, the format of which is given in this chapter.

UNDERSTANDING DIRECT QUOTATIONS AND PARAPHRASING

In Step 5, an example was given of the correct use of a direct quote from the book, *Children with Tourette Syndrome: A Parents' Guide*, as well as an example of paraphrasing and plagiarizing the same material. The plagiarism was considered so because the writer used the same material but changed it slightly in order to make it her own. Even some of the same wording was used. In addition, the writer did not note where the material came from; she did not give credit to the author. Paraphrasing, however, is not the same as plagiarism. It means you have put the material you have read in your own words and not the words or style of the writer. It means you have thought about the quotation, you want to retain the sense of the writer, and yet you want to say it in a way that fits your paper better or is more understandable to you. The paraphrase may be almost the same length as the author's, but it generally is shorter.

To demonstrate the difference between an exact quote and a paraphrase of the same material, a direct quote from *Ryan: A Mother's Story of Her Hyperactive/Tourette Syndrome Child* is given here, as well as a paraphrase and a plagiarized account of the same material. Note that, with the paraphrase, a reference is given showing where the material came from, just as with the direct quotation; otherwise, it would be considered plagiarism. Quotation marks are not used because it is not a direct quotation.

Direct Quotation from *Ryan: A Mother's Story of Her Hyperactive/Tourette Syndrome Child*

There was one particular day at school that was especially rough for Ryan. He had been having problems keeping his behavior and tics under control that day and a few of the other students, in their childish ignorance, seized the opportunity to tease and make him miserable. Not wanting to let down his "tough guy" exterior, Ryan kept the hurt inside until he got home. Then like a flooding river, the tears began to flow and the pain he was feeling began to ebb its way out. 'Why Mommy, why,' he cried. 'Why do I have to have this? . . . I HATE this stupid Tourette Syndrome! I just want to be a REGULAR kid' (95–96).

Paraphrase of Quote from *Ryan: A Mother's Story of Her Hyperactive/Tourette Syndrome Child*

Ryan had many days at school that were rough, but one in particular stands out. He tried to keep his hyperactivity and his tics under control, but he had been having more troubles than usual on that day. Some of his schoolmates, noticing his difficulty, grabbed the opportunity to tease him, making him feel worse. When he got home, he started crying and venting his frustrations to his mother. Over and over he sobbed, 'Why Mommy, why,' he cried. 'Why do I have to have this? . . . I HATE this stupid Tourette Syndrome! I just want to be a REGULAR kid' (95-96).

Note that, with the paraphrase, the idea is there, but the words are different. The description of Ryan's frustrations with his problems is shown, just as with the direct quotation, but the words are not given exactly as in the quotation. Even so, page numbers are given at the end of the paraphrase to show where the material can be found. The following example shows how the same paragraph could be plagiarized.

Plagiarism of Quote from *Ryan: A Mother's Story of Her Hyperactive/Tourette Syndrome Child*

There were many rough days Ryan had at school trying to keep his hyperactive behavior under control as well as his tics. Some of the kids at school saw him making weird noises, so they thought that a good opportunity to make fun of him. They taunted him and made his life miserable all day. He didn't want them to know how he felt, so he kept it inside. When he got home, he began to weep uncontrollably. Finally, he cried out to his mother, "Why do I have to have this? I DESPISE having Tourette! I just want to be a NORMAL kid!"

There is no page number or citation after the plagiarized paragraph. It is presented as if the material is the writer's own words, not from the book by Susan Hughes, which is why it is considered plagiarism. If the writer had put the parenthetical notation (95–96) after the paragraph or had introduced it earlier in the paper as coming from Hughes' book, then it would not have been considered plagiarized. Avoiding plagiarism is as simple as that—giving credit to the person who wrote the material and not claiming it as your own.

Using Brackets within Citations and Other Alternative Sources

This is a good place to note another kind of citation—the use of the parenthesis within a parenthesis. It involves placing square brackets by hand around the material, if such marks are not available on your word processor or typewriter. Square brackets are used primarily for two reasons: for clarification of what has been said previously and to indicate an ellipsis in the middle or end of a quotation to show something has been left out. When brackets are used to provide an explanation, the explanation is brief so as not to disturb the train of thought.

Another alternate type of citation with parentheses is the use of *sic*, a Latin abbreviation meaning "thus" or "so." It is also used for two reasons: to indicate the word preceding it was spelled that way in the quotation and to indicate emphasis of your own.

The following examples will help you see how to use both square brackets and parentheses.

Examples with Brackets

1. TS patients retain a clear consciousness during paroxysms [sudden attacks] and therefore are aware of making noises and grimacing, which frightens some people.

2. The MayoClinic Web site says, "We have to be accepting of people with TS, rather than making them pariahs. [. . .] We have to make reasonable accommodations for them in school and at work."

Note that the second sentence is closed with a period, but the ellipses show something has been left out. A space is given before the three dots for the ellipsis. Brackets come between the first and second dot and after the final dot. If, however, the ellipsis occurred at the end of the quote, the punctuation would look like the following [. . .]. (ellipses, then the bracket, and a final period for the end of the sentence).

Examples with Parentheses

3. Carpenter says, "Chad seemed unable to control his attacks of cuprolalia [sic] in public places."

   [The word "coprolalia" is not spelled correctly; hence the word "sic" is used.]

4. The Web site KidsHealth for Kids emphasizes that "even though a kid with Tourette Sydrome can get better as he gets older, he will always have it. But it *won't make him sick or shorten his life*" (emphasis added).

ADDING REFERENCES TO YOUR PAPER

Having considered how to use the material you have researched, you now need to learn how to give credit. The most popular style, which is used in this manual, is called the MLA style and is taken from the *MLA Handbook for Writers of Research Papers,* Fifth Edition (1999). While there are other research formats for referencing, such as the APA or American Psychological Association style used for psychology and the University of Chicago style used for history, most English instructors use the MLA form. The *MLA Handbook* uses parenthetical notation for referencing and a Works Cited page at the end of the paper to show more detailed bibliographic material of the sources. A discussion of parenthetical notation is given in this step, while information concerning the Works Cited page is given in Step 10. Familiarize yourself with both, and you can correctly insert the references in your paper.

Inserting Parenthetical Notation

Parenthetical notation means exactly what the term implies—notations are within parentheses indicating where the material was taken from. While this form is straightforward to use, keep in mind that the way you cite the material in parentheses must correspond to the documentation in the Works Cited page. For example, if you cited Susan Hughes because you quoted or paraphrased some material from *Ryan: A Mother's Story of Her Hyperactive/ Tourette Child,* you would list her in the Works Cited page with other bibliographic information about the book. Since the information on the Works Cited page is listed in alphabetical order, her entry would appear as "Hughes, Susan."

With parenthetical notation, it is important to be as brief as clarity will permit. Only the information needed to identify the source is necessary. Usually, the first time you quote from an author, you will use the person's name in introducing the quote. If the quotation is introduced by the author's name, then it is not necessary to repeat the author's name in parentheses after the quote. Only the page number or numbers need to be included. If the quotation is not introduced, however, you should cite enough of the reference in parentheses after the quote to identify the source. Also remember that the reference should follow the quotation as soon as possible. Rules and examples follow to show how this is done.

Books with Author or Editor. Use the author's last name or the name of whomever begins the Works Cited entry, such as the editor or translator. Follow the name with the page number or numbers without using any punctuation.

```
(Hughes 39)
```

If two or three authors are given, list all authors in the citation. If more than three authors are given, use the abbreviation *et al.* after the first name, which means "and others."

```
(Smith and Johnson 103)
(Quinn et al. 56)
```

Two or More Works by the Same Author. If you use two or more works by the same author, add all or part of the title, underlined, between the author's name and the page number.

```
(Barclay, Romans 49)
```

Multivolume Works. If citing from more than one volume of a multivolume work, include the volume after the author's name, followed by a colon and the page number or numbers.

```
(Archer 2: 2012-23)
```

Literary Works. If citing a literary work, give information other than or in addition to the page numbers. For example, the citation for a play would include the act, scene, and line(s).

```
(King Lear 5.5.8)
```

The Bible. References to the Bible are similarly cited, giving information other than or in addition to the page number—for example, the book, chapter, and the verse/s. You may omit, however, page numbers when citing complete works.

```
(John 1.1-5)
```

Works Listed Only by Title. If no author or editor is given, use a shortened version of the title of the work.

```
(Report on Indian Education 3)
```

Complete Works. When citing a complete work (such as referring to a book as a whole), the work is usually introduced in the context. However, even if you do not introduce the work, page numbers are not required (see the following example). In addition, one-page articles or articles in works that are organized alphabetically, such as encyclopedias, do not require page numbers in the notation.

Examples

```
1.  Reference to a whole book: (The Unwelcome
    Companion)
2.  Reference to a multivolume work that has not been
    introduced: (Barclay, vol. 2).
3.  Reference to dictionary entry ("Tourette," def. T).
```

Citing Indirect Sources. It is best to give the direct or original source when possible, but sometimes the indirect source fits better with your paper and may be the only account you have to verify your conclusions. When that happens, if you are actually quoting a quotation or paraphrase, put the abbreviation *qtd.* which stands for "quoted in" in parentheses after the quote.

```
"As difficult as the physical discomfort can be to
deal with, I think the most damaging part of Tourette
Syndrome is its emotional impact" (qtd. in Hughes 250).
```

Citing a Quotation within a Quotation. The same rule applies when citing a quotation within a quotation as with citing indirect sources. The parenthetical reference is placed where a pause would naturally occur (preferably at the end of a sentence), as on the following page.

Summer says, "After the great period of Old Testament prophecy closed, the Jews fell into difficult times (3). 'It was such troublous times as these that gave birth to apocalyptic literature'" (Allen 15).

Electronic Sources. Page numbers are not required for nonprint sources, such as electronic or CD-ROM sources, because usually none are available. For a document on the World Wide Web, the page numbers of a printout are not normally cited because the pagination could vary from printout to printout. If, however, the source does include fixed page numbers or section numbers (such as numbered paragraphs) cite those numbers, using *pars* for "paragraphs." The *MLA Handbook* suggests that if the source has no page numbers or any other kind of reference numbers, the work should be cited in its entirety. The important point is to give enough of the citation so that it can easily be found on the Works Cited page.

Examples

1. An article concerning Tourette Syndrome in the MayoClinic database states that "one of the most important things in dealing with TS is establishing a prompt, accurate diagnosis, particularly in childhood" (par. 5).

   With this example, because the title of the article and the database are given in the citation, there is no need to give further information. The complete listing will be given in the Works Cited at the end of the paper. You will notice, however, that the material came from paragraph 5.

2. Bagheri, Kerbeshian, and Burd point out that "Once believed to be rare, Tourette's Syndrome is now known to be a more common disorder that represents the most complex and severe manifestation of the spectrum of tic disorders" (par. 1).

   The three authors presented the article, "Recognition and Management of Tourette's Syndrome and Tic Disorder" to *American Family Physician* using the Searchbank InfoTrac. Since their names are given, it is unnecessary to give further documentation in the citation.

3. Raenna Peiss in <u>The Tourette Syndrome Chapter</u>
    <u>WebRing Site</u> points out four diagnostic criteria for
    Tourette Syndrome, a neurological disorder charac-
    terized by tics (par. 1).

    The citation on the Works Cited page will include the full information,
    beginning with Raenna Peiss who owns the Web site. Note, however, that
    the material came from paragraph 1.

4. The Carpenter's home page is "dedicated to all who
    have helped us gain back some of our sanity after
    this devastating **THING** took over our lives."

    The home page will be cited in its entirety on the Works Cited page,
    giving information concerning how to access it. The citation will begin with
    Carpenter, R. David who owns the page.

When using parenthetical notations, remember that the citation should
not interfere with the readability of the paper. One way to make the paper
more readable is to introduce the quotation or reference within the text of
the paper. This is often done by using verbs that blend in with the flow of
the paper. Listed here are ten possible ways to introduce a quote by R. David
Carpenter from his home page; there are many others. You will notice they
are all introduced by verbs.

1. Carpenter says, "...
2. Carpenter points out ...
3. It is easy to see that Carpenter is referring to ...
4. Carpenter agrees with ...
5. Carpenter writes that ...
6. Carpenter discusses ...
7. Carpenter believes that ...
8. Carpenter explains his view by ...
9. Carpenter suggests that ...
10. Carpenter notes that ...

You may have noticed that only the first example, using the word "says,"
includes a comma after the introduction. This example uses a comma
because, after the word "says," a direct quotation from the home page will
follow. The other examples do not require commas to make the quotation
flow within the sentence. There are other words that could be used as well as

these to make a smooth transition into the body of the paper. By introducing the quote, however, the paper becomes more readable and is easier to document. Only the page number or numbers need be included in the parentheses after the quotation.

A different style is used for a long quotation of more than four lines that is set off from the text. A colon introduces the quotation, and the parenthetical citation comes at the end of the quote after the period. A long quotation is indented ten spaces on the left and is double-spaced. No quotation marks are used, because the indentation indicates that the material is quoted. The following example is used in the Tourette paper.

Example

It would be wrong, though, to say that other family members are not affected, as Nick, Ryan Farrell's little brother, says:

> Sometimes I feel mad at my family because Ryan gets so much of the attention. I know my family loves me, but I still get mad at Ryan's Tourette because if he didn't have it, he wouldn't get the attention of our mom and dad. I also get mad at Ryan's Tourette because sometimes he isn't very nice to me. He says he's sorry when he's mean to me, and most of the time I forgive him. I love my brother, even though it's hard, so I put up with his Tourette. (Fowler 107)

The instructions for parenthetical notations may seem hard to remember at first, but they are easier than you may think. They are simple common-sense methods for letting the reader know where to find the sources you used, pointing directly to the sources on the Works Cited page. They fall into two main categories. The first category involves those quotations and paraphrases that have been introduced and only need a page number in the citation in parentheses. The second category is those quotations or paraphrases that are not introduced that require the author's name along with the page reference in parentheses.

Quotations should always be brief and to the point, except when you want to present more to the reader than is possible in four lines, as in the case of how Nick feels about being the brother of one who has Tourette. They are meant to support your research, not constitute the bulk of your paper. When too many are used, the reader may find them cumbersome.

They indicate that you have not assimilated the material yourself. Quotes are used to show your research skills and to show how other people agree with your thinking. They are necessary for a research paper, but keep in mind to use them economically rather than to overuse them.

EXERCISE 1   Quoting and Paraphrasing

Select a fairly lengthy paragraph from an article in an electronic source or from another reference source concerning the topic you have chosen for your research. Copy the paragraph into your notebook as an example of a direct quotation. Then try your hand at paraphrasing the quotation. Trade paraphrases with a classmate and check each other's paraphrasing.

EXERCISE 2   Check for Plagiarism

From the paragraph you paraphrased in Exercise 1, compare your paraphrase to the original quotation. Let your partner check to see if you have used your own words or if you have plagiarized the quotation. Explain your findings to each other.

9

Writing the
First Draft

The first point to remember as you write your first draft is the method you will use for citing your sources. This manual uses what is known as the MLA style, which calls for parenthetical notation—noting within parentheses the source you have used.

In the previous step, you were given detailed instructions about how to put parenthetical notations in your paper. The examples provided in this section use parenthetical notations. They record the essential information for finding the source in the Works Cited page at the end of the paper. Seeing how they are used in these examples will help reinforce the rules in Step 5.

WRITING THE FIRST DRAFT

When you begin to write your paper, sort your note cards and/or note sheets into piles according to the divisions of your outline. Because you already know the major and minor points of your paper, you can then incorporate the information from the cards in your paper in the right place. As you use the material from each card, you may want to draw a big X on the card to indicate that it has been used.

It is likely you will be using a word processor; if so, you can delete what is not needed and add material as you write. If you are writing your paper manually, a helpful hint is to write on one side of the page only. That way you can see what you have written without having to turn the pages from back to front.

Since you will be using parenthetical notations, you will need to record where you got the information on your rough draft. If you do not want to include the complete information at this point, simply abbreviate the source and then put a number on the note card to indicate this was the first source you used, then the second source, and so on. It may be easier to use a different color pen to highlight the information so that it will stand out. You can fill in the complete information in your next draft. The information will essentially be the author's last name and a page reference of where you obtained the material. If you got the information from the Internet, you will record the title of the article or name of source and page, if given. Then you will give the complete documentation at the end of your paper on the Works Cited page.

While the *MLA Handbook* prefers parenthetical notation (the method used in this manual), some instructors may require a different kind of documentation, using endnotes or footnotes instead of parenthetical notation. Complete information on how to use endnotes and footnotes is given in Appendix C. It is never acceptable to use both kinds of referencing in your paper. You must use one method or the other; they cannot be combined.

Perhaps you are wondering how to write your paper. There are several methods, but your thesis should be the clue as to how you will develop it. For example, the thesis in the paper concerning Tourette Syndrome has two distinct divisions. The first part shows that Tourette has often been misdiagnosed by the medical field and is misunderstood by the general public; the second part shows the effects of that misunderstanding on the person with Tourette as well as others associated with the person. Even though the completed paper in Appendix A uses the Quotation Introduction approach, the following discussion shows how each type of introduction can be used with the Tourette paper, using the same thesis.

WRITING THE INTRODUCTION

There are many ways to write an introduction. Five distinct ways are given in this discussion, and you can usually find your paper fitting into one or more of these categories. The important point to realize, though, is that your introduction sets the tone for the paper. It creates interest in your reader and makes it clear you have adequately researched your material. Because of this, carefully consider how you are going to develop the introduction.

In addition, the introduction for your research paper will be longer than only one well-developed paragraph as used in essay writing. You may need two or three paragraphs to introduce your topic. In determining how to write your introduction, you may also want to consider how you are going to develop your paper. Methods for developing your paper are discussed later in this step.

Before discussing the five methods for your introduction, be aware there are some styles to avoid in introducing your topic. Humorous or "cutesy" introductions are out of place for a research paper. It is not likely that a research paper will be humorous; save humor for a process essay, a personal experience essay, or a classification essay. Sometimes, however, beginning writers like to introduce their essays by asking questions. This is rarely done effectively, but if this style is used with any paper, the questions must be answered within the essay. Asking questions to introduce a research topic is a style best avoided.

The most feasible types of introductions are the inverted pyramid or funnel approach, short anecdotes, the outline or summary approach, quotations (that may also include definitions of key words or phrases), and comparison/contrast or comparison only. A combination of these is also possible. Quotations, for example, are possible with almost any form.

Following is a description of each of these types of introductions, accompanied by a sample introduction that could begin the Tourette paper, which is included in Appendix A. Consider each of these types carefully before writing your paper to see which one fits best with your research.

Using the Inverted Pyramid or Funnel Approach

The inverted pyramid or funnel approach is probably the easiest method to use, especially if the purpose of your paper is persuasive. When you think about it, however, most research papers are persuasive in that you want to get your points across regarding the research you have done, and you want your reader to agree with you. With the inverted pyramid or funnel method, you begin your introduction with general, broad statements, then work down to the thesis, which is the last statement of the introduction.

The following introduction uses this format. You can see that it begins with a broad, general statement about Tourette Syndrome and then points out the need for public awareness of the disorder.

The next paragraph continues to work down to the thesis, which has been italicized for your benefit. As you read the completed paper in Appendix A, note how this introduction could have been used instead and that it would have worked as well. Keep in mind the broad first statements that work down to the narrow thesis at the end of the introduction, and you can see how this method works.

Example: Inverted Pyramid or Funnel Introduction

Tourette Syndrome, a disorder affecting some 200,000 people in the United States, was first diagnosed in 1885. It still remains, however, a mystery to most of the general population and is often misdiagnosed by those in the medical field. It is a debilitating illness causing involuntary movements and sounds that are often repulsive to those who do not understand what is happening. According to the National Organization for Rare Disorders, Tourette also has no known cure, affecting boys four times more than girls (3). It is bad enough to have the disorder, which is obvious, but to face the repercussions from others is even worse. Some with the disorder have been disowned by family members, fired from their jobs, or expelled from their schools because of lack of understanding and support.

As the twenty-first century dawns, it would seem that a disorder affecting so many people would be accepted more, but the truth is that little is known about the disease except by those who are affected. Such little study has been made of Tourette by the medical field and by associated groups that few are aware of what it is and how to deal with it. They often treat the individual for symptoms of other diseases, which only aggravates the problem. *Because of the frequent misdiagnosis of Tourette Syndrome by physicians or psychologists and the lack of information by the general public, the person with Tourette too often has severe problems that also affect those associated with him or her.*

Using the Short Anecdote Approach

Using anecdotes is another way to introduce your paper. People sometimes think anecdotes have to be humorous (and some are), but anecdotes, simply defined, are accounts of interesting incidents or events. Sometimes these are found in newspapers; they may be human interest stories of people with unusual occupations or interests, or they may be stories of something that happened a long time ago. Often they give narratives or details about historical figures that make their lives more interesting. Anecdotes make the research paper more interesting because they stimulate the reader to want to know more about what you are writing. If they are used effectively, anecdotes are an excellent way to introduce your paper.

Example: Short Anecdote Introduction

Often the child with Tourette Syndrome will exhibit symptoms of hyperactivity when only a few months old, thus causing the parents to think their child is simply unusually active. As parents look back, though, they can see a pattern of behavior that indicated something more than just hyperactivity. Susan Hughes describes in her book about her son Ryan the difficulty she and her husband had with trying to cope with Ryan's compulsive behavior, fits of rage and violence, and his complete lack of control at times. She tells of going to one doctor only to have the doctor tell her that their son had a neurological disorder known as Minimal Brain Dysfunction. Another neurologist told them their son had Attention Deficit Disorder with Hyperactivity; a pediatric psychiatrist said they were doing all of the "right" things and their son was just more active than usual and, with medication, could be helped.

In spite of one medication after another, however, their son was too often totally out of control, shrieking

at the top of his lungs for no reason, and, without
warning, spitting and cursing. Then afterward, he
would "lay his head against my shoulder as if to say,
'Do something, Mommy. I can't help it'" (Hughes 76).
The Hughes family felt that no one seemed to know what
to do. Their case is not unusual. *The misunderstanding
of Tourette Syndrome by physicians or psychologists
and their frequent misdiagnoses along with the lack of
knowledge of Tourette by the general public often
causes severe problems for the person with Tourette
as well as those associated with him or her.*

Using the Outline or Summary Approach

Using the outline or summary approach in the introduction acquaints your
reader with what you will discuss in your paper. Of course, you are not really
outlining the introduction; you are simply letting the reader know what your
paper is about and the major points you will discuss. You are familiar with
this format because your instructor has probably told you when writing essays
to tell the reader what you will write about in the introduction, then write
about it in the body of the essay, and finally tell the reader what you have
written about in the conclusion. The outline or summary approach follows
this format.

An introduction using this approach to the paper about Tourette
Syndrome begins by identifying the problem, then informs the reader what
to expect in the paper: that Tourette is a complex problem that is often misdiagnosed, that society has little understanding of the disorder, and because
of these two things, in particular, everyone suffers—the person who has the
illness as well as those around him or her. It concludes with the thesis, which
is italicized again, so that you can see how the outline or summary approach
would be as effective for the Tourette paper as other types of introductions.

Example: Outline Introduction

It is believed that Tourette syndrome is more common than once thought and that it affects as many as one
in 2,000 people, according to "A Story of Tourette
Syndrome" (3). The reason that some people do not know
that they have Tourette is that it does not interfere
with their lives. Often people do not realize they have

Tourette because they do not have all of the classic symptoms. They think they are dealing with a problem like their Aunt Susie's or Uncle Bill's and that it is just an hereditary trait. Too often the medical profession misdiagnoses the problem as Attention Deficit Disorder with Hyperactivity or a neurological disorder known as Minimal Brain Dysfunction or even that the child is just strong willed. It seems they do not know what is going on. Rick Fowler recalls being in a consultation room with five or six doctors and a couple of other medical professionals who looked at him as if he had wasted their time. Their comment was "Son, we've checked everything we can think of. There's nothing that we can find physically wrong with you. You just need to calm down" (13).

The public in general is also unaware of what is happening with the person afflicted to cause the obnoxious behavior and inappropriate language, at times treating the person as an outcast. This, of course, has an adverse effect on the person who has the disorder and has a domino effect on his or her caregivers. *It is clear, then, that the misunderstanding of Tourette Syndrome by physicians and psychologists and their misdiagnoses of the disorder along with the lack of knowledge of Tourette by the general public often causes problems for the individual with Tourette as well as for those associated with him or her.*

Using the Quotation Approach

Using pertinent quotations in the introduction can also be an effective way to start your paper. While quotations may often be a part of other types of introductions, as you have seen in the sample funnel approach and the anecdotal approach, they can also be used almost exclusively. The writer of the paper feels that the quotations very succinctly say what his or her paper is about and, therefore, this is the best approach to use. Often with this type of introduction, key words or phrases are defined or identified because of their importance to the paper.

The paper on Tourette Syndrome in Appendix A uses this approach. Words and phrases used in the introduction that indicate some of the symptoms associated with the disorder are *clicking sounds*, *repetitiveness*, *impulsiveness, ceremonial fashion of saying "one…two…three" and concluding with 'done.'*

Example: Quotation Introduction

"I thought maybe I was crazy," Stacy said in "A Mother's Quest for Answers." "I went through eight doctors. They told me, 'She'll grow out of it.' I knew she wasn't in control, and I told them that. But nobody would listen to me" (1). This is the account of one mother's quest for answers concerning her daughter's constant clicking sounds, her repetitiveness, and her impulsiveness. Another account is similar. David Carpenter said he and his wife "returned from a trip to the Caribbean to find their son Chad had started pushing his upper teeth against his lower teeth with such force as to cause root damage and bleeding." He writes, "He did it in ceremonial fashion, speaking the words, 'one . . . two . . . three,' and concluding by loudly saying DONE." That night "they spent in the hospital emergency room only to end up hearing several doctors agree they had never seen anything like it" (1). Jim Eisenreich, outfielder with the Kansas City Royals, says, "I was bounced from one doctor to another and was treated for problems that I didn't have. [. . .] Finally, I was eventually diagnosed correctly, and proper treatment now allows me to live a normal life" (Foreword). Tracy Haerle, editor of <u>Children with Tourette Syndrome: A Parents' Guide</u>, says she and her husband consulted "an endless stream of physicians" before they were able to get the kind of help they needed after their son began showing symptoms at the age of two and a half (vii).

Statements like these could be repeated over and over because of the difficulty in diagnosing Tourette Syndrome or the lack of knowledge on the part of some in the medical field. According to Rick Fowler in <u>The Unwelcome Companion</u>, "Misunderstanding has plagued Tourette Syndrome sufferers since long before the disorder had its name" (17). *This misunderstanding of Tourette by physicians and psychologists and their misdiagnoses of the disorder along with the lack of knowledge of Tourette by the general public often causes problems for the individual with Tourette as well as for those associated with the person.*

Using the Comparison/Contrast or Comparison Approach

The comparison/contrast or comparison approach is a method that effectively shows how two or more similar or dissimilar ideas will be presented in your paper. In comparing, you show the similarities of ideas, people, or objects; when contrasting, you show the differences without the similarities. Not all papers lend themselves to this type of introduction. With a little thought, however, you may find this an effective method for letting the reader know what your paper is about.

As you can see from the sample introduction that follows, Tourette Syndrome, even though diagnosed more than one hundred years ago, can be compared with a newer diagnosed disorder, Chronic Fatigue Syndrome. Less information is given about Chronic Fatigue Syndrome in the introduction, of course, but it is clear from the introduction that there are some similarities and dissimilarities with Tourette.

Example: Comparison Introduction

Syndrome is a word used to describe an illness or disorder that is known because its symptoms are considered characteristic of a particular disease. There are many syndromes identified in the medical field, but two that affect the general public perhaps more than others are Tourette Sydrome, or TS, and Chronic Fatigue Syndrome, or CFS. Both of these syndromes are debilitating, and both are mysterious. That is where most of the similarities lie; however, the differences are manifold. For example, Tourette Syndrome is known to be genetic, whereas according to the Web page, "Chronic Fatigue Syndrome," from Yahoo! Health, Chronic Fatigue Syndrome has no known cause. Some believe it to be caused by a virus or enterovirus, or from a compromised immune system. Tourette Syndrome has no cure; while some with CFS do return to normal within five years, others become dramatically worse (Schweitzer 1). The symptoms of Tourette Syndrome are highly visible with vocal and motor tics, while, according to Yahoo! Health, the symptoms of CFS are much like those of common viral infections such as muscle aches, headache, and fatigue. In addition, treatment for Tourette Syndrome consists of medications to calm the person. Currently, no treatment has proven effective with CFS, which has resulted in only treating the symptoms ("Chronic Fatigue Syndrome," Yahoo! Health).

Tourette Syndrome and Chronic Fatigue Syndrome do share many similarities and differences, as shown, but one of the most interesting points about the two disorders is that with TS there seem to be feelings of guilt or resentment or embarrassment. With CFS there is none of this, only sympathy and encouragement. *Possibly the difference is the misunderstanding and misdiagnoses of Tourette by physicians and psychiatrists coupled with the lack of knowlege of TS by the general public that causes problems for the person with TS as well as those around him or her.*

As you can see from the examples, all five types of introduction are viable options for the same paper. The quotation approach was chosen for the final paper (see Appendix A), but any one of the five would have been as effective. They all blend into the thesis, which blends into the rest of the paper.

When you write your introduction, keep in mind that the conclusion should relate to it in some way. After reading about the different ways to write the conclusion, you can decide which one works best with your introduction.

Because your research paper is your own thinking, except when documented, you *do not* need to use such phrases as the following:

"In this paper, I will ..."
"In this paper, I have ..."
"I believe ..."
"I think ..."

These phrases only weaken your paper. They are signs of a beginning writer; you want your writing to be more sophisticated. It is also unnecessary to use personal pronouns because your paper is written objectively. Leave out *I, me, my, mine, we, us, our*, and the indefinite pronouns *you, your*, and *yours*. Use third person pronouns as much as possible: *he, she, it, him, her, its, they, their*, and related forms.

One Student's Introduction

One student, Mona Tyson, was given the general subject of the heath in British literature. After careful study, she narrowed her topic to include Emily Brontë's *Wuthering Heights*, Shakespeare's *King Lear*, and Thomas Hardy's *The Return of the Native*. Her research was commendable. Her introduction and conclusion are found here, and her total paper appears in Appendix B at the end of this text. As you can see, her introduction used the inverted pyramid or funnel approach. She used broad statements and worked down to her thesis, which is italicized. The purpose of her paper is to show how the heath plays a part in the lives of the characters in the works, both realistically and symbolically.

```
Each geographical region around the world, whether
large or small, continent or country, has a portion of
land within its boundaries that overpowers and domi-
nates all others. Examples are the dry, dusty deserts
of Africa, the swamplands of Louisiana, and the extreme
conditions of Siberia in Russia. These vast and dis-
tinctive areas possess individual characteristics that
enable each to overwhelm its inhabitants, surrounding
lands, and oftentimes nature itself. The previous
```

examples give an idea of the role that the heath plays in <u>Wuthering Heights</u>, <u>King Lear</u>, and <u>The Return of the Native</u>.

Harold Bloom quotes Hardy in <u>Modern Critical Views</u>:

The face of the heath by its mere complexion added half an hour to evening; it could in like manner retard the dawn, sudden noon, anticipate the frowning of storms scarcely generated and intensify the opacity of a moonless midnight to a cause of shaking and dread. (<u>Views</u> 22)

According to Thomas Hardy, author of <u>The Return of the Native</u>, the heath is a barren land, occupying space as far as the eye can see, whose inhabitants look out upon it in the darkest hours of the night feeling trapped, never to escape, wondering about the world beyond (56).

Not only Hardy, but also Emily Brontë and William Shakespeare have their own thoughts about the heath. Even though their styles and interpretations differ slightly, it is evident through the selected works that Hardy, Brontë, and Shakespeare share the same feeling. *They emphasize the effect the heath has on the lives of their characters by directly associating it with the characters and their surrounding conditions.*

GETTING INTO THE BODY OF THE PAPER

Sometimes it is difficult to know how to move from the introduction to the body of your paper. You are undecided about whether to use a con paragraph or a summary or biographical material. The discussion that follows should help you learn how to move smoothly from one part to the other.

Using the Con Paragraph

In Step 6, which had to do with forming a thesis, you learned that a good the-sis always has an antithesis, which may or may not be stated. This is especially useful in persuasive writing, and while the purpose of your research paper may not be totally persuasive, you will want your reader to consider your point of view. Therefore you would do well to consider the opposite point of view.

If you decide to state some of the opposing points, your con (or opposite) paragraph would come immediately after the introduction. It would begin with transitions that show your admission or concession. Such transitions as "it is true that," "admittedly," "certainly," "it is a fact," "while it is evident," and "undoubtedly" are excellent beginnings for con paragraphs. A list of transitions is given in Step 11, pages 136–137.

An example from the paper on Tourette Syndrome shows how a con paragraph works. If it were to be used, it would be the paragraph immediately following the thesis. The antithesis is italicized to show that it was only a part of the con paragraph.

Example: Con Paragraph

While it is true that sometimes Tourette Syndrome is identified immediately, too often the contrary is true, causing resentment and heartache for all who are affected. It is also true that some in society are aware of Tourette Syndrome and therefore know how to react to the disorder, but the majority of the public is not edu-cated about this disorder. This, too, causes problems for the person with Tourette and for those associated with the person.

This paragraph helps you see that the writer is secure in her thinking that a better diagnosis needs to be made of Tourette and that the public needs to be aware of the problem because of the effect it has on the person with the disorder. Through this paragraph, she shows that she has stronger points to make than the antithesis. As it stands, the con paragraph really serves as a transitional paragraph, making the transition from the thesis to the body of the paper smoother than just "jumping into the paper." If you use the con paragraph, you are ready to write the body of your paper and need to decide how best to do it.

On the other hand, you may have decided not to use a con paragraph with a stated or implied antithesis, and you want to develop your paper in another way. There are other options, but again there are definite points to consider.

Using Transitions

The first point to consider in moving into the body of your paper is to make a smooth transition from the thesis to the rest of the paper. A transitional word or phrase at the beginning of the paragraph makes the paper read more smoothly.

For example, one student used the following as her thesis:

```
Accordingly, Shakespeare's plays Julius Caesar,
Coriolanus, and Antony and Cleopatra are unparalleled
illustrations of how overambition and intrepidness
lead to the downfall of a political figure and are
still important examples of secular effigies today.
```

She then moved easily into her next paragraph with the following:

```
        With that in mind, it brings about the question,
"Why did Shakespeare have such a great influence on lit-
erature?" The answer is that at that point in history,
his style and characterizational methods were considered
radical and eccentric.
```

The second paragraph continued from there. This excerpt shows you how she moved into the paragraph by using the traditional phrase "With that in mind."

It is important, then, to make a smooth transition from the thesis to the rest of the paper, no matter how you develop the paragraph. Refer to the list of appropriate transitions for use in making your paper read more smoothly on pages 136–137 in your text. You should find the exact transition you need.

Using a Summary

Suppose, however, you feel that it is very important to write a short summary of the work or works you have read in order to adequately discuss them in your paper. Soon after the introduction is the place to form a succinct summary. It should never be the bulk of your paper; if it is, your instructor will immediately be alerted to the fact that you have done little research and that all you are really doing is using the summary as a filler. You need to be very careful at this point not to plagiarize as well. It is very easy to use the author's words and claim them as your own. That is wrong!

Using Biographical Material

The same guidelines hold true for material concerning the author's life. If the author's birthplace, dates, family, education, or other biographical information are not significant and have little to do with your thesis, do not include them just to fill up space. If you do use this kind of information, there is no need to reference facts that are considered common knowledge or knowledge anyone would know without having to do research.

In the two literary papers in Appendices B and C, you will note that neither paper records anything about the authors of the works about which the researchers were writing. The reason was that information about the writers and their backgrounds was irrelevant to the research paper. Again, had it been included, it would have been superfluous.

DEVELOPING THE BODY OF YOUR PAPER

After you make the transition into the body of your paper, the next question you are faced with is exactly how to develop your paper. There are many ways to do this. Choose the one that works best for you, depending on what you want to do in your paper and how you have developed your thesis.

There are six distinct methods you can use to develop your paper. You may also use a combination of any of the six, using one method for developing the main points and another for developing the minor points. Consider all of the ideas given here to determine the best method for your paper.

Using Chronological Order

Anything that is in *chronological order* is done in order of time. With this method, you would trace events backward or forward. This form is particularly suited for biographical or historical studies. It is also beneficial for explaining technical processes that involve sequential steps, making it useful in scientific studies and in almost any research that demands order in development. For example, if you were writing a paper on space, you could well begin with the first space capsule that orbited the earth and go from that point to include high points in space activity, including the walk on the moon and linking with Russian satellites. This would be done in chronological order, or time order, of how things were done in space.

Using Spatial Order

Spatial order is exactly what its name implies—organizing according to space. This is an effective method to use in researching an area. For example, if you were researching dialects in the United States, you might want to organize them into sections of the country. Or if your social studies instructor assigned you to investigate voting patterns in a particular area and write about them, this would be a good method to use. Perhaps your biology class is doing a project on why frogs develop three legs rather than four in a particular area. You could use spatial order because it would cover different areas of the country.

Using Cause and Effect Order

Cause and effect order is a higher level of critical thinking, a technique that is encouraged in research. It involves the problem-solving techniques of starting from the cause and then looking to the effects that caused such a result, or beginning with the effects and working back to the cause. With this format, you are using either an inductive or a deductive approach. You would use logical reasoning with the process of an argument or *syllogism* that includes a major premise and a minor premise, with a conclusion that may or may not be stated. The syllogism may simply be understood, but the rationale is evident in your ability to develop the paper. The Tourette Syndrome paper uses this approach. A syllogism for the paper might look like the following:

Major Premise: Many physicians and psychiatrists do not understand Tourette Syndrome; thus, they often do not diagnose it properly.

Minor Premise: The general public has little knowledge of Tourette Syndrome, causing the child with Tourette not to be accepted.

Conclusion: Because many physicians and psychiatrists do not diagnose Tourette Syndrome properly and because the general public does not understand Tourette, the child with the disorder suffers as well as those associated with him or her.

You can see from this deductive process how the syllogism works. The paper will be built on this deduction.

Using General to Particular Order

General to particular order can be used when you want to start from a broad generalization and then support it with details. An example might be from F. Scott Fitzgerald's *The Great Gatsby*, in which he showed the 1920s as a fun-loving, carefree time with very little seriousness. You could support this idea with details from the book and perhaps some of his other writings to show how this was portrayed. Another example might be research into the Y2K problem that was feared by many people. You would start off with the generalization that the Y2K problem, expected to play havoc with everything from operating a dishwasher to flying a jet, was caused by the hysteria of the computer age, not the end of the world at the end of the millenium. Then you would point out the basic reason for the hysteria—the inability of computer microchips throughout the world to read the date of the year 2000, instead reading 1900. Next, you would detail the steps that were taken to avoid such a catastrophe.

Using Particular to General Order

Particular to general order is the opposite idea of general to particular. Using this approach, you begin with examples and build to the climax. You conclude with a broad generalization summarizing the particulars, pointing to their significance. This is similar to what is done with a persuasive paper: you state the thesis, give examples and support while building to your final, strongest point, and then move on to your conclusion.

Sara Popham's paper about Byron's heroes based on Milton's Satan appears in Appendix C. She uses the particular to general style of writing because she begins with examples and builds to the climax or the final assumption that "Byron based his heroes, not just on a common Romantic theme, but on Milton's Satanic hero in particular, attempting to restate the beliefs that he felt Milton had alluded to only vaguely in *Paradise Lost*."

As stated earlier, the methods for developing the body of your paper can be combined, and Sara does this, as she must. She identifies ways in which Byron's Lucifer and Milton's Satan were similar, but then she comes to her conclusion based on examples she has found in both Byron's and Milton's works.

The body of the paper does not have to be as rigid as one, two, three, but it will take some shape if you plan carefully.

Using Comparison/Contrast or Comparison

The comparison and contrast method is another technique that uses higher level thinking skills. First, of course, you must know material of two different natures in order to make the comparisons and/or contrasts. From this knowledge, you would come to a general conclusion by showing the similarities and/or differences. You develop this conclusion into a thesis that involves a look at both works or ideas. A comparison/contrast paper could be written using works of literature about the same subject, time periods that are similar or dissimilar, or authors of similar stature. This method could be employed with almost any subject, whether literary, historical, or scientific.

Appendix B contains Mona Tyson's paper, in which she uses the comparison and contrast technique. Her thesis clearly shows that she is going to compare and contrast the three writers—Emily Brontë, William Shakespeare, and Thomas Hardy—and their works. She moves first to Brontë's *Wuthering Heights* and demonstrates how Brontë develops the heath and the feelings of the characters toward the heath. The paper then moves to Shakespeare's *King Lear,* showing how he stresses the effect of the heath on the characters. Mona finishes with Hardy's *The Return of the Native* and shows how his characters are affected by the heath. The comparison and contrast method was most effective for this paper because Mona analyzed three works.

WRITING THE CONCLUSION

If you have planned well for your introduction and conclusion, they will fit together like the pieces of a puzzle. Your conclusion ties together or finalizes what you have written, just as your introduction interested the reader in what he or she was about to read. Your conclusion shows the reader that you have presented your material in such a way that he or she agrees with your argument. Or it shows that you have done an adequate job of describing the voting patterns as noted earlier or the development of space as shown by the time order you used. Your conclusion should fit smoothly with the rest of the paper so that it flows well rather than stands out as a separate entity.

As with the introduction and the body of the paper, you may develop the conclusion in several ways. The conclusion generally is no longer than one or two paragraphs; it is needed simply to draw your paper to a close. Several methods for writing a conclusion and examples of each, using the Tourette paper, are listed here. Consider all of them to determine the one that best fits your paper.

Restating the Thesis

Restating the thesis and then broadening out the subject is a familiar way to conclude your paper. This is the opposite of the funnel type of introduction. In effect, by using this method your paper would resemble an hourglass. The introduction begins with broad statements and concludes with the specific thesis, while the conclusion restates the thesis, then broadens out with general statements. Restating the thesis means not using the same words as the thesis but making reference to the thesis so that the paper fits smoothly together.

As you can see from the following example, the conclusion begins with the restated thesis, which was narrow, then broadens out with a quote indicating that having Tourette doesn't have to limit the individual; he or she can obtain goals in spite of this handicap.

Tourette Syndrome, as shown in this paper, has many
negative effects. Part of the reason has to do with the
difficulty in diagnosing the disorder at the onset of the
illness and then in its not being accepted by others.
This causes problems for the TS sufferer and for his or
her family. It is clear that the key to acceptance lies
in educating the public, because kids with Tourette are
no different from other kids. Tics do not make them different inside. "In fact, some famous people who have
Tourette do some pretty cool stuff—like Philadelphia
Phillies outfielder Jim Eisenreich. . . Denver Nuggets
guard Mahmoud Abdul Raulf, and the real—life brother of
Neve Campbell, an actress of the TV show *Party of Five*
("A Story of Tourette Syndrome" 3).

Summarizing the Main Points

Summarizing the main points is another effective way to conclude your
paper. This method works well with the outline or summary introduction. In
your introduction you told the reader what you were writing about; in your
conclusion you are telling the reader what you have written about. This is
also an easy way to conclude your paper because you are writing a very short
summary of your paper.

The following example shows how a conclusion using this method would
fit into the Tourette paper if the outline or summary approach were used in
the introduction.

As shown, then, Tourette Syndrome has repercussions for everyone involved. The problem, however, is
compounded when physicians and psychiatrists fail to
recognize the disorder. This often brings more feelings
of frustration on the part of parents who are trying to
cope with the problem and on the child who doesn't
understand what is happening. Even those outside the
family often offer little support, sometimes seeing the

problem as lack of discipline or "lazy parenting." The key, it seems, is to bring about more awareness of the disorder in the general public and more acceptance of the child who is no different except for his or her tics.

Emphasizing Key Words or Phrases

Emphasizing key words or phrases is another possibility for concluding your paper, especially if the terms were used in your introduction. The words or phrases should be those that stand out as you think about your paper. They bear repeating in the conclusion because of their importance. This format works well with the introduction that uses key words or phrases as shown in the example quotation introduction with the Tourette paper.

As you can see, the conclusion is centered around words that were repeated throughout the introduction: *crazy, clicking sounds, repetitiveness,* and *impulsiveness.*

Example: Emphasizing Key Words or Phrases

As unnerving as the problem of Tourette is for the family as well as the child who has Tourette, the person with TS should not be looked down upon by society. In "Meeting Someone with Tourette's Sydrome" from the MayoClinic Web site, the note is made that "Only rarely are you likely to enounter someone with the more dramatic kinds of tics associated with Tourette Syndrome [. . .]. Simply put, if the person has TS, he's not 'crazy,' he simply has a treatable neulogical condition and there's no reason to feel threatened" (1). The clicking sounds, repetitiveness, and impulsiveness are only symptoms of the disorder and are made involuntarily. The person with Tourette, therefore, deserves the encouragement and support of everyone.

Using a Succinct Quotation

Using just the right quotation can be an effective way to draw your paper to a close. You may find a quotation that fits well with one you might have used in the introduction, or you may choose another that says what you want to say. Using a quotation helps the reader feel you have spent time searching for the exact quote to sum up your paper.

The following example uses a different quotation from the one in the introduction, but it draws together the points made in the paper. It also fits well with the last paragraph before the conclusion in the paper in Appendix A.

Example: Using a Succinct Quotation

It is clear, then, that the person with Tourette Syndrome has difficulties that often seem insurmountable, but it doesn't have to be like that. Rick Fowler says:

While researchers do biological battle with Tourette Syndrome, the average person can help the cause of Tourette Syndrome by educating others. One source of the disorder's power is its ability to humiliate and embarrass its victims to the point of ruining their social and professional lives. If the public could become accepting enough to make such humiliation obsolete, a great deal of the disorder's strength would disappear. TS will likely always be a disruptive neurological problem, but it need not be a socioeconomic handicap. (109)

These four ways to conclude your paper are effective if you put some thought into how your paper fits together as a composite whole. There may be others, however, that you find just as acceptable. Whichever method you use should show a finality to your paper and should fit well with the introduction. Your conclusion shows the reader that you have completed your findings and that you have presented them convincingly.

The final example is from Mona's paper. Note which type of conclusion she uses and how it relates to her introduction. (See pages 178 and 189.)

It is also obvious, after extensive research, that the characters and their circumstances are directly affected by the heath in Wuthering Heights,

<u>King Lear</u>, and <u>The Return of the Native</u>. The heath
proves itself to be an invincible foe against anyone
or anything that steps into its mighty walls. It is
even personified as possessing human qualities. Bloom
best describes the heath in all three works as being
"slighted, enduring, obscure, obsolete, and superseded
by none" (<u>Interpretations</u> 122). After close analysis,
it is evident that the heath, that massive stretch of
wild and desolate land, possesses power and strength
beyond the imagination.

Mona began by restating her thesis in the first sentence of the conclusion, which is parallel to the way she introduced her paper. She included a quotation for emphasis, just as she did in her introduction. She then broadened her statements out to the final sentence, which further emphasized the power of the heath. Mona was effective with her conclusion because of its evident finality. Clearly, this was the end of her paper; she brought it to a close.

Following these directions will guide you in writing your first draft. As you are writing your paper, make sure that you add in your references so that you will have no problem when you have finished your paper and begin the next step, Compiling the Works Cited Page.

EXERCISE I   Write an Introduction

I. In the exercises in Step 7, you made a tentative outline of the research paper on which you are working. Now you are ready to begin the writing process. For this exercise, look back at your thesis statement and then decide which of the five kinds of introductions would be most appropriate. Write a tentative introduction for your paper.

2. As a class activity, divide into pairs. Have your partner look at what you have written and determine if the introduction you wrote fits well with your thesis or if another type of introduction would be better.

EXERCISE 2 _____ Write the Body

Continue with your partner and refer to the outline you made for your paper. Look back through Step 9 and decide which format would be the best way to develop your paper. Write out the order you have chosen and state why you think you could develop your paper best by using that format. Consult your partner to see if he or she agrees.

EXERCISE 3 _____ Write the Conclusion

Continue with your same partner. Go back over what you have done so far and then write a tentative conclusion. After you have written it, determine which form you chose based on the information in this step. Discuss with your partner whether you have chosen the best form.

STEP

10

Compiling the Works Cited Page

The Works Cited page contains information about each of the references you used. Sources that you consulted and rejected should not be included, nor should you list references that you did not cite in your paper.

The Works Cited page appears at the end of your research paper and gives complete information about where you found your material. You have already compiled this information on your source cards. Simply organize your cards in alphabetical order according to the author's or editor's last name, then record all of the bibliographic material. The few rules necessary for compiling the page are given here, and examples are given for each of the sources you will probably use.

COMPILING THE WORKS CITED PAGE

The following guidelines will help you in putting together your Works Cited page:

1. Entries begin at the left-hand margin with the subsequent lines of the entries indented five spaces (or half an inch). All entries are double-spaced. This is called a hanging indent; most software programs allow this to be done automatically.

2. All works are listed in alphabetical order according to the author or editor's last name.

3. If there is no author or editor, begin with the title of the work. Note that the words *the*, *a*, and *an* are not alphabetized when they begin a title.

4. Do not number the entries on the Works Cited page.

5. Do not give page numbers except for works in anthologies, periodicals, and newspapers. Also, abbreviate all months except May, June, and July.

6. If there are more than three authors, list the first one and add *et al* ("and others") instead of listing everyone's name. The name of the first author is in reverse order with the last name first; subsequent authors' names are in normal order with the first name first. Use *and* to separate the names if there are two names; if three names, separate the second name by a comma then put *and* between the second and third names.

7. When two books by the same author are cited, use three hyphens in the second entry instead of the author's name. Alphabetize these entries according to the titles of the books, following rule 3 above.

8. Use the following initials to indicate when information cannot be found: *n.p.* for no place of publication; *n.p.* for no publisher; *n.d.* for no date of publication; and *n.pag.* for no page if none is given. Put these initials in the place where such information is usually found.

9. If a suffix, such as *Jr.*, or a Roman numeral, such as *IV*, appears after the author's or editor's name, it should be preceded by a comma.

```
Hollandale, Jerry R., IV

Jones, James, Jr.
```

10. The essential information for all entries includes the author, the title of the work, the place of publication, the publishing company, and the copyright date. With some sources, such as periodicals, additional information will be needed. The examples given after this list show variations of the form to accommodate different sources. By following these examples, you should be able to cite any entry; ask your instructor if you run into an unusual source.

11. Step 4 gives a detailed listing of the style to be used in citing sources on the World Wide Web. Examples are also given in the listing that follows.

EXAMINING SAMPLE ENTRIES

Print Sources

Book by One Author

Fowler, Rick. <u>The Unwelcome Companion: An Insider's</u>
     <u>View of Tourette Syndrome</u>. Cashiers: Silver Run,
     1996.

Note: The title of a book should be underlined, but the punctuation following the title should not be underlined.

Two or More Books by the Same Author

Orwell, George. <u>Animal Farm</u>. New York: Harcourt, 1946.

---. <u>1984</u>. New York: Harcourt, 1949.

Two Authors

Bykofsky, Sheree, and Jennifer Basye. <u>The Complete</u>
     <u>Idiot's Guide to Getting Published</u>. New York:
     Alpha, 1998.

Two Authors with the Same Last Name

Kirk, Clara M., and Rudolf Kirk. <u>William Dean Howells</u>.
     New York: Twayne, 1962.

Editor but No Author

Fisher, Patricia, ed. <u>Age Erasers for Women: Actions</u>
     <u>You Can Take Right Now to Look Younger and Feel</u>
     <u>Great</u>. Emmaus: Rodale, 1994.

Two Editors or More Than Two Editors

Note: Treat these in the same way that two authors or more than two authors are handled, using "eds." after the editors' names.

No Author or Editor Given

<u>Louisiana Migratory Game Bird Hunting Regulations</u>
     <u>1999-2000</u>. Baton Rouge: Dept. of Wildlife and
     Fisheries, 1999.

Note: Do not alphabetize by *a*, *an*, or *the*.

Pamphlet

<u>Report on Indian Education</u>. Washington: American
     Indian Policy Review Commission, Task Force Five,
     1976.

Note: A pamphlet is treated as a book with the title, then the source information.

The Bible

<u>The NIV Study Bible: New International Version</u>.
     Kenneth Barker, gen. ed. Grand Rapids: Zondervan,
     1985.

Note: In the parenthetical notation, the title of the book of the Bible, the chapter, and verses would be included with <u>The NIV Study Bible: New International Version</u> coming before the chapter and verses the first time it is used. After that, only the book's title, chapter and verse(s) are used.

Work in an Anthology

Gray, Thomas. "Elegy Written in a Country Churchyard."
     <u>England in Literature</u>. Ed. Helen McDonald, John
     Pfordresher, and Gladys V. Veidemanis. Glenview:
     Scott, Foresman, 1991. 314-15.

Dictionary or Encyclopedia Article

LaSor, William Sanford. "The Dead Sea Scrolls." <u>The New
    International Dictionary of the Bible</u>. Eds. J. D.
    Douglas and Merrill C. Tenney. Grand Rapids:
    Zondervan, 1987.

Note: If no author is given, begin with the title of the article. Also, when citing a familiar reference book, do not give full publication information. List only the edition (if stated) and the year of publication.

"Migrants." <u>The Encyclopedia Americana</u>. 1993 ed.

Introduction, Preface, Foreword, or Afterword

Eisenreich, Jim. Foreword. <u>Children with Tourette
    Syndrome: A Parents' Guide</u>. By Tracy Haerle.
    Rockville: Woodbine, 1992.

Multivolume Work

Wester, Janet. "The Return of the Native." <u>1300 Critical
    Evaluations of Selected Novels and Plays</u>. Ed. Frank
    N. Magill. 3 vols. Englewood Cliffs: Salem, 1978.

Note: Cite the total number of volumes if you use all of them. In the parenthetical notation, the specific reference to volume and page number should be given. For example, (2: 101–2).

   If you are using only one volume of the set, include the bibliographic information for that volume. Only the page reference needs to appear in your parenthetical notation. If the volume has an individual title, cite the book without reference to the other volumes in the set.

Barclay, William. <u>The Revelation of John</u>. Philadelphia:
    Westminster, 1960.

Newspaper Article

Blanchard, Kevin. "People Learn to Conquer Fear of

Slithery Creatures." The Advocate [Baton Rouge]

23 May 1999: B1+.

Note: If the city is not included in the title of the newspaper, include it in brackets (not underlined) immediately after the title of the paper. If the article is continued on an additonal page, simply put a plus sign and include the exact page in the parenthetical notation.

Anonymous Article

"Moments of Serenity." American Way 1 Nov. 1995: 201.

Note: If no author is given, cite the reference with the title, excluding initials and *a, an,* or *the* when alphabetizing the entry. This includes newspaper and/or periodical articles.

Periodical Article

Gay, Peter. "Sigmund Freud." Time 29 Mar. 1999: 66–69.

Note: If the article had been continued later in the magazine with other articles intervening, only the plus sign is used with the page reference.

Review in a Newspaper or Periodical

Brown, DeNeen L. Rev. of Something's Wrong With Your

Scale, by Van Whitfield. Sunday Advocate Magazine

[Baton Rouge] 1 Aug. 1999: 26.

Nonprint Sources

Personal Interview

MacDonald, Michael David. Personal interview. 5 Aug.

1999.

Interview Broadcast on Television or Radio

Gumbel, Bryant. Interview with Dick Morris. The Early

Show. CBS. WAFB, New York. 7 Dec. 1999.

Television or Radio Program

"Sacred Arias in Rome." Great Performances. Perf.

Andrea Bocelli. WLPB, Baton Rouge. 7 Dec. 1999.

Film or Video

The Alamo. Dir. John Wayne. Perf. John Wayne, Richard

Widmark, Laurence Harvey, and Chill Wills. MGM,

1960.

You've Got Mail. Dir. Nora Ephron. Perf. Tom Hanks, Meg

Ryan. Videocassette. Warner Bros. Videocassette,

1998.

Note: Videos, cassettes, videodiscs, slide programs, and filmstrips are cited like films except that the original release date is given if applicable. The medium (videocassette, videodisc, slide program, and so on) is also included before the name of the distributor.

Performance

Carousel. By Richard Rodgers and Oscar Hammerstein. Dir.

Shirley Pourciau. Perf. Maxie Schexnayder, Chris

Garrett, Nancy Adler, John Miller. Lee Theater.

Baton Rouge. 9 Nov. 1975.

Speeches or Oral Presentations

Kennedy, John F. "Inaugural Address." U.S. Capitol.

Washington, D.C.: 20 Jan. 1961.

Government Documents

United States. House of Representatives. Conference
Report on H.R. 3194, Consolidated Appropriations
Act, 2000. 17 Nov. 1991.

Electronic Sources

Periodical Publication on CD-ROM, Diskette, or Magnetic Tape

Clark, J.K. "Complications in Academia: Sexual
Harassment and the Law." <u>Siecus Report</u>. 1994. 25+
CD-ROM. SIRS/SIRS. 13 June 1995.

Note: Since this material came from a printed source originally, the page
number (25+) is given.

Nonperiodical Publication on CD-ROM, Diskette, or Magnetic Tape

United States. Dept. of State. <u>Patterns of Global
Terrorism</u>. CD-ROM. Washington: National Trade Data
Bank, 1996.

Hayes, Jane. <u>Hamlet</u>. By William Shakespeare. Diskette.
New York: Scholastic, 1989.

Online Databases

Through an Online Service

"Tourette Syndrome: A Mother's Quest for Answers."
<u>KidsHealth.org For Parents</u>. America Online.
14 July 1999 <http://www.kidshealth.org/parent//
behavior/tourette.html>.

Bagheri, Mohammed, et al. "Recognition and Management of
Tourette's Syndrome and Tic Disorders." <u>American
Family Physician</u> 15 Apr. 1999 v59 i8 p2263 (1).
<u>InfoTrac: Health Reference Center</u>. 13 July 1999
<http://web2.searchbank.com/itw/session/>.

Through a Computer Network

Bruun, Ruth Dowling, et. al. "Guide to the Diagnosis and
Treatment of Tourette Syndrome." Tourette Syndrome
Assoc. <u>Internet Mental Health</u> 1997. 7 July 1999
<http://www.mentalhealth.com/book/p.40-gtor.html>.

"Chronic Fatigue Syndrome." adam.com. <u>Yahoo! Health</u>
1999. 21 July 1999 <http://health.yahoo.com/
health/Diseases-and-Conditions/Disease...
Chronic-fatigue-syndrome>.

Note: The information required for an online database source is the
author (if available), the title of material (in quotation marks), the title
of database (underlined), the publication medium, the name of the computer service, and the date of access. If you cannot find some of the information, cite what is available.

Personal or Professional Site

"Tourette's Syndrome: Startling Behaviors that can be
Disconcerting." 3 March 1997 <u>MayoClinic Health
Oasis</u>. Mayo Foundation for Medical Education and
Research. 14 July 1999 <http://www.mayohealth.
org/mayo/9703/htm/tourette.htm>.

Carpenter, R. David. Home page. 13 July 1999
<http://www.citynet.net/personal/chad/index1.html>.

Abbreviations for Publishers' Names on the Works Cited Page

Shortened forms of publishers' names immediately follow the cities of publication, making it easier for the reader to find the works you have used. Keep in mind, however, these rules:

1. Omit articles (*a, an,* and *the*), business abbreviations (*Co., Corp., Inc.*), and descriptive words (*Press, Publishers*). When citing a university press, include the abbreviation *P* because the university may publish independently of its press.
2. If the publisher's name includes the name of one person, cite the last name alone. If the publisher's name includes the names of more than one person, cite only the first of the last names.
3. If the publisher's name is commonly abbreviated with capital initial letters and if the abbreviation is likely to be familiar to your readers, use the abbreviation as the publisher's name (*MLA*). If it is likely your readers will not know the abbreviation, shorten the name according to the guidelines above (*Mod. Lang. Assn.*).

Abbreviations for Titles of Literary and Religious Works

1. In documentation, you may abbreviate the titles of works and part of works; however, it is best to introduce an abbreviation in parentheses immediately after the first use of the full title in the text: "In Hamlet (Ham), Shakespeare . . . ."
2. Abbreviating titles is appropriate if you repeatedly cite a variety of works by the same author.
3. Works of well-known authors may be abbreviated by a shortened form of the title (MkT for *The Monk's Tale* by Chaucer; Od. for Homer's *Odyssey*).
4. For biblical references, you may abbreviate the names of the books of the Bible (Gen. for Genesis, Heb. for Hebrews). Exceptions are those with four or fewer letters, which should be written out entirely (Ruth, Ezra, Acts).

EXERCISE 1   Compiling the Works Cited Page

Compile a Works Cited page of the sources that you already have for the paper you are working on. Get with a partner so that each person can check the other's sources to determine if they are correct before you type your final copy.

11

Revising Your Paper

By now you have written your first draft, added the parenthetical notations, and used your source cards to list your sources on the Works Cited page. Even though the major part of your paper has been completed, you still need to proof your paper for errors and then revise it for better style, structure, and organization.

Proofing your paper means looking at it from an outsider's point of view and making the changes necessary to have a really good paper. Reading your paper out loud can be a good way to "hear" how your research paper sounds. It is as if another person were listening and finding places that need additional work.

First Reading: Checking for Content, Organization, Clarity, and Referencing

The best way to proof your paper is to read your rough draft several times in order to catch any errors you have made. Reading it at least three times before preparing the final copy is a good guideline. Each time you read it, look for specific items. That way you do not have to spot every error at once. After you have found the errors, correct them and begin the revision process.

Checking your paper for content, clarity, and organizational structure is the first step in proofreading your first draft. Have your outline in hand for this reading. Since you carefully planned the organization of your paper when you prepared your outline, check to see if your paper fits the points on the outline or if you have overlooked a topic you meant to discuss. Reading for content also allows you to see whether your paper is in the right order and whether you have given adequate treatment to major points. If you find gaps in your paper after this reading, you may need to add or delete parts to be more in keeping with your planned outline. You may need to revise your outline if, in your research, you were unable to support the points you thought you would cover in your initial planning.

In addition to checking content, this reading helps you see if you have made your points clear to the reader. Since you have spent a great deal of time in your research, what seems clear to you may not come across that way to the person reading your paper. Clarity is absolutely necessary in order not to obscure the meaning and content of your paper. Sometimes just a restructuring of your sentences is all that is necessary to keep your information from being ambiguous.

While checking your paper for content, make sure that your references are properly noted and that you have included all of the necessary information on the Works Cited page. This is also a good time to verify that all sources cited in your paper are noted on the Works Cited page. After all, a research paper is what its name implies—research—finding out what other people have to say about your topic and documenting their comments. You want to be certain that you include all of your references. At the same time, with this reading, make sure that you have only listed sources that you used.

This first reading provides the background for the other two readings since, if any additional information needs to be added or if anything needs to be deleted, it can be done before checking for grammar and punctuation.

Second Reading: Checking for Grammar and Style

With this reading, you will be concerned with *how* you wrote your paper. Look for grammatical errors: sentence fragments, run-on sentences, comma splices, pronoun usage, misplaced modifiers, wordiness, and tense shifts. When writing about a literary source, keep in mind that you should use the present tense; write as if the work were being written now. For example, write "Fowler notes that he does not allow the Tourette demon to dominate his thoughts but instead his goals and dreams come first."

During this reading, also note the use of personal pronouns and avoid them. While some instructors allow a less formal approach to research and thus allow personal pronouns, more sophisticated writing uses the objective point of view. In other words, don't use the pronouns *I, me, my, mine, we, us, our,* and *ours.* Use the third person pronouns: *he, she, it, they, him, her,* and *them.* Also delete the pronouns *you, your,* and *yours.* These are unnecessary in a research paper because they are indefinite pronouns; save their usage for process or how-to papers.

Additionally, this second reading is a good time to look at the flow of your paper, especially the use of transitions or transitional devices. If your writing seems too disjointed or lacks continuity, you may need to find ways to make it read more smoothly by using transitions within sentences and by connecting your paragraphs with transitional words or phrases. Study the following list of transitions to help make your paper flow better. Also, use your thesaurus to find synonyms to substitute for words that are repeated often instead of using the same words over and over. You will be doing your reader a favor as well as learning new words yourself.

Finally, a careful reading can help you identify weak sentences and faulty sentence structure as well as problems with paragraph development. A good guide to judge a well-developed paragraph is to find the topic sentence, then check the paragraph for support and note the way it concludes. A paragraph should contain only one idea. Paragraphs that are too long are difficult to comprehend, just as paragraphs that are too short are difficult to follow.

You might want to use one of the many computer applications available to check for grammatical errors. For example, Grammar Check allows you to find such errors as subject/verb agreement, sentence fragments, run-on sentences, and so forth. You need to understand, though, these applications do have their limitations. One advantage, however, is that you can use the Find/Replace command to look for common problems you might have. In that way, you can catch errors you commonly make and will learn to avoid them in future writing.

While the second reading may not require as much time as the first reading, it is a necessary part of revision. Checking your paper for grammar and being sure that you are consistent with style is vital to a well-written paper. Research is all but meaningless if it is recorded in such a way that the reader cannot follow the content and/or has difficulty determining what you are saying because of your grammar and the flow of your paper. It is a good idea to have a fellow student proofread your paper at this point to help check for errors you might not see.

USING APPROPRIATE TRANSITIONS

The following transitions can help you make your paper read more smoothly. By no means are they all of the transitions possible, so don't think you have to confine yourself only to these. You should judge each transition carefully, however, to find the ones most suitable for your paper.

Argument or Concession

admittedly, certainly, consequently, furthermore, in fact, it is true that, nobody denies, obviously, of course, on the other hand, the fact remains, undoubtedly

Cause and Effect

accordingly, because, since, thereafter, thus, whereas

Condition

even though, if, in case, nevertheless, on condition that, therefore

Connectives

additionally, after, again, also, and, as well as, before, besides, formerly, finally, further, addition to, last, later, next, not only. . . but also, previously, since, then, too, first, second, third, and so on

Differences

although, but, even so, however, in spite of the fact that, on the contrary, on the other hand, otherwise

Similarities

as, like, likewise, resemble, similar to, just as

Emphasis

absolutely, certainly, especially, extremely, importantly, undoubtedly

Example

for example, for instance, thus, to illustrate

Place

above, alongside, below, beyond, everywhere, here, near, under

Summary

finally, in conclusion, lastly, therefore, thus, to sum up

THIRD READING: CHECKING FOR SPELLING, PUNCTUATION, AND CAPITALIZATION

This final reading is a must because the research you have done will be clouded if your paper is filled with errors in spelling, punctuation, and capitalization. Therefore, take one last look at your paper objectively to find these errors. You do this by reading one sentence at a time.

Look over your paper for the words you often misspell. Usually, you will misspell them again. Using the dictionary can help you with this check; keep it by your side as you write. If a word looks wrong, it usually is. Your instinct often tells you that it is time to take a closer look and reach for the dictionary. If you are truly a poor speller, ask someone else to read your paper and help you find errors in spelling. Of course, there are computer applications that help in this area, such as Spell Check. However, Spell Check is not a foolproof way to determine if you are saying what you want to say. For example, it cannot tell if you are using the word *their* when you want to use *there*, or *bear* for *bare*, or other homonyms. So be cautious about relying on Spell Check completely. You might end up saying something entirely different from what you meant to say.

While you are reading your paper for spelling errors, check for punctuation errors as well. Too little punctuation or too much punctuation can harm the flow of your writing. If you have questions about how to use commas, quotation marks, and periods, refer to the punctuation checklist given here. It shows rules and examples for almost any problem you might have.

Finally, check for capitalization errors. Usually, these errors are inadvertent. You thought you remembered to capitalize the name, city, or street, but you may have overlooked it. In this last reading, pay particular attention to capital letters. Keep in mind that proper names, languages, religions, historical events, periods of time, documents, governmental bodies and departments, titles—of books, articles, reports, poems, plays, short stories, and newspapers—names of television and radio programs, the Deity, the Bible, and property adjectives all begin with capital letters.

This last reading, while shorter than the other two, is a must if you are to have a well-written paper. If errors in spelling, punctuation, and capitalization are frequent, they obscure the research you have done because the reader has to constantly work through the errors. The following information will help you determine whether you have used correct punctuation.

FOLLOWING RULES FOR PUNCTUATION.

The rules given here are by no means all of the rules of punctuation; however, they are ones you will likely encounter in writing your research paper. After each rule, an example of its usage is given to guide you in making the applications.

Using Apostrophes

1. Use an apostrophe to indicate a contraction—two words put together in a shortened form; however, in the research paper, contractions are discouraged.

2. Use an apostrophe to show ownership:

   ```
   Annabelle's research was well done.

   The boys' caps were engraved with their team's
   emblem.
   ```

   Note that *boys' caps* indicated that all of the caps belonged to the boys individually while *team's emblem* is collective, referring to the team as a whole.

3. Do not use an apostrophe to form the plural of a number:

   ```
   Her SAT score was in the high 1400s, qualifying her
   for a scholarship.

   My grandparents lived in the 1800s.
   ```

4. Do not use an apostrophe to form the plural of an abbreviation:

   ```
   MDs        VCRs

   PhDs       RNs
   ```

Using Brackets and Parentheses

1. Use brackets around the word *sic*, which means "thus," to indicate an error in the quoted sentence.

   Shaw admitted, "Nothing can extinguish my interest
   in shakespear" [sic].

2. Use brackets around material that has been added to a quotation to clarify a sentence.

   "The commissioner [Fay Vincent] ordered George
   Steinbrenner to give up day-to-day control of the New
   York Yankees . . ." (Matthews 116).

   In this case, the name Fay Vincent was added to make sure the reader knows which commissioner is meant. The parentheses show the parenthetical notation.

   "Echolalia is a bothersome tic because often other
   people are offended by having their words repeated,
   but it is involuntary and cannot be helped (contrary
   to what some people think)."

   The explanation within the parentheses helps the reader understand the fact that echolalia is a part of the disorder of Tourette Syndrome.

Using Colons and Semicolons

1. Use a colon to introduce a long quotation.

   Dr. Larry Burd, a specialist in dealing with Tourette
   Syndrome, understands that children with Tourette
   have difficulty in school. He comments:

   Many children with Tourette Syndrome have academic
   difficulties not because they cannot do the work,
   but because they cannot complete it. [. . .] This
   could be due to tics, attentional problems, or

```
obsessions or compulsions. Often it is helpful to
break the work up into shorter segments. For exam-
ple, instead of giving a child twenty math problems
to solve, give him seven, five, or three at a time,
several times a day. Then, as his work habits
improve, the teacher can increase the number of
problems she gives him each time. (177)
```

Note: Two other rules are noted with this example. Ellipses are used to indicate a part of a sentence has been left out, and the end punctuation is shown for parenthetical referencing—a period ends the quotation; the reference is then given in parentheses.

2. Use a colon to introduce a list of words.

```
The special at Jay's Barbecue includes the following
dinners: ham, pork ribs, chopped beef, chicken, and
sausage.
```

3. Use a semicolon to join two clauses of a compound sentence without a conjunction.

```
Etymology is the study of words; entomology is the
study of insects.
```

Using Commas

1. Use a comma before the conjunctions *but, and, for, yet, so, nor,* and *or* only if the clause that follows can stand as a complete sentence.

```
Maria asked me to go to the movie, but I already had
plans for the evening.
```

2. Use a comma in a series of three or more.

```
Kendra, Jim, Ellen, and DarEllen have been friends
since elementary school and now plan to go to the
same college.
```

3. Use a comma to separate groups of three digits of numbers (hundreds, thousands, millions, and so on).

Tomás paid $23,500 for his car.

4. Use a comma after an introductory phrase or clause.

After the last hurricane in Florida, people evacuated quickly when the weather report showed another hurricane coming.

5. Use commas to set off the year in dates.

My next doctor's appointment is August 22, 2001, which is also my wedding anniversary.

6. Use a comma to enclose contrasting expressions.

Congress, not the President, has the power to declare war.

7. Use commas to enclose appositives together with their modifiers.

The Tasmanian devil, a ruthless marsupial, will attack and overcome creatures much larger than itself.

8. Use commas to separate lines of an address in a running text.

Mr. Patel listed his address as 2224 Longbeach Street, Lemoore, California 93245.

9. Use commas to set off a direct quotation. The comma precedes the quotation marks.

Ryan Farrell's mother says, "Ryan not only has to deal with the everyday frustrations of growing up and going to school, but he deals on a daily basis with ridicule, embarrassment, and total frustration."

10. Use commas before and after a nonessential modifier.

```
The airplane, having lost one of its engines, landed
safely.
```

Using Ellipses

Use ellipsis points to indicate an omission in a quotation. Three dots separated by spaces indicate an omission; a fourth dot is added if the omission precedes or follows a period. In MLA style, brackets are used with ellipses to indicate that the ellipses were not part of the original quotation.

```
In his book, On Death and Dying, Billy Graham
describes an archaelogical dig in China depicting
death as a battleground. "A ghostly imperial guard
of more than seven thousand life-size clay soldiers
[. . .] standing in battle formation to protect the
grave of China's first emperor. [. . .] Their horses,
harnessed in gold and silver, lay in a pit near the
tomb" (213).
```

Using Hyphens

1. Avoid ending a typed line with a hyphen if the sentence continues on the next page.
2. Always hyphenate between syllables and between double consonants when they come at the end of a line.

```
The doctor said he would never be wil-
ling to operate without your consent.
```

3. Do not hyphenate a word if only one letter is left at the end of the line. Begin the next line with a complete word. For example, do not hyphenate *a-board, e-mancipate,* or *u-topia.*

Using Periods

Use a period at the end of a statement or a command.

```
The family was disappointed that the house did not
sell.

Close the door, please, when you leave the room.
```

Using Question Marks

Use a question mark after a direct quotation, but not after an indirect question.

```
Did you find the book I was reading?

He asked if I had found the book I was reading
interesting.
```

Using Quotation Marks

1. Insert quotation marks around the titles of poems, essays, short stories, chapter headings, periodical articles, and songs. Examples are "A Red, Red Rose" (poem); "Of Parents and Children" (essay); "Tickets, Please" (short story); "Working with More Than a File—A Document" (chapter heading); "Don't Let It End This Way" (magazine article); and "Rhapsody in Blue" (song).

2. Use quotation marks around direct, short quotations. The quotation does not have to be dialog. The punctuation used with quotation marks, however, varies according to the type of quotes.

```
Mr. Blackburn said, "Your son is the best swimmer on
the team."

"Your document is not complete," said the instruc-
tor, "unless you have given proper credit to the
author."
```

Note: The period appears *inside* the quotation marks in both examples. The comma is also *within* the quotation marks in the second example indicating that the thought is interrupted.

"Julius Caesar was the foremost Roman of his day and perhaps the most powerful man in the known world" (534).

Note: With parenthetical notation, the period is *after* the parentheses, not within the quotation marks. With long quotes, however, the period comes before the parenthetical notation.

Fowler declared, "A developing cycle of obsessions, compulsions, tics, embarrassment, rejection, shame, frustration, and depression can create a whirlpool of despair!"

Fowler, then, declares war on his "whirlpool of despair"!

Can you understand why Fowler declares war on his "whirlpool of despair"?

Note: With the first example concerning Fowler's statement, the exclamation point is included *within* the quotation marks to indicate these were his words. With the second example, the exclamation mark comes *after* the quote because it is not a complete quote but it emphasizes his feelings, which is a part of the quotation. The third example asks the question of whether the reader understands Fowler's position and is not a part of the quoted material.

As in these examples, all punctuation marks, such as semicolons, colons, questions, and exclamation points go outside the closing quotation mark except when they are a part of the quoted material.

3. Long quotations consisting of four lines or more are set off from the rest of the paper by indenting ten spaces from the left margin. The quotation should be double-spaced. No quotation marks are needed because the indentation indicates the quote.

   In addition, if you quote only a single paragraph or part of one, do not indent the first line more than the rest. However, if you are quoting two or more paragraphs, indent the first line of each paragraph three spaces or an additional quarter of an inch. If the first sentence quoted does not begin a paragraph in the source, do not indent it the additional amount. The research papers in the appendices contain examples.

4. Quotation marks are added around a part or all of a single line of poetry within the text. Two or three lines may also be incorporated within the text by using a slash with a space on each side (/) to separate them.

```
"I'll not weep that thou art going to leave me, /
There's nothing lovely here" ("I'll Not Weep" 381).
```

5. For quotations of poetry more than three lines long, set the quotation off by indenting ten spaces from the left and double-spacing the lines.

```
Wordsworth's poem, "It Is a Beauteous Evening,"
expresses his feeling of being at one with nature:
        It is a beauteous evening, calm and free,
        The holy time is quiet as a Nun
        Breathless with adoration; the broad sun
        Is sinking down in its tranquillity; (309)
```

Using Underlining

Underline titles of books, plays, newspapers, long poems, films, paintings, and ships. If you use a word processor that identifies italics from Roman type enough, you may prefer to italicize these titles instead of underlining them. Ask your instructor which method he or she prefers. Examples include The Red Pony (book); Antigone (play); The Washington Post (newspaper); Paradise Lost (long poem); Mona Lisa (painting); USS Kidd (ship).

MAKING THE FINAL REVISIONS

After you have finished the three readings—checking for content, organization, clarity, and referencing; checking for grammar and style; and checking for spelling, punctuation, and capitalization—you not only know your paper inside and out, but you have also done what is necessary for a good paper. You have learned what you have done wrong and how to go about revising it. Revising it, then, is the next step. You probably made some revisions while you were reading your paper; now is the time to complete your revision.

You want to be proud of the finished product. Besides producing a better paper because you have corrected your errors, you have become a better writer in the process. By learning and using these three techniques, you can soon become your own best critic as you read and revise and then read and revise again.

EXERCISE 1　　　　　Revising

Working in small groups or with a partner, read through the paper that you have written so far. First, check to see if you are satisfied with the content and organization of each other's papers; then check for clarity, sentence structure and grammatical errors. Finally, reread each other's papers for errors in spelling, punctuation, capitalization.

STEP

12

Preparing the Final Copy

You have now followed every step throughout this guide and have made the necessary revisions. You are ready to complete your assignment. This last step gives final instructions regarding the mechanics of your research paper and the order in which your instructor will probably want it turned in. By following these directions, you will not hand in a less-than-perfect paper after all of your hard work.

UNDERSTANDING THE MECHANICS OF THE RESEARCH PAPER

1. Use white bond paper, 8 1/2-by-11 inches. If you use computer paper, make sure to tear off the edges before turning in your paper; however, most printers are now laser or ink jet printers and do not have the notched edges.

2. Double-space your paper throughout, including quotations and the list of Works Cited.

3. Keep your margins consistent. Except for page numbers, leave one inch on both sides and one inch at the top and bottom unless your instructor suggests otherwise. Do not justify the type on the right margin if you are using a word processor.

4. Indent the first word of a paragraph five spaces from the left margin. Indent long quotations of four lines or more ten spaces from the left margin.

5. According to the *MLA Handbook*, no cover sheet is required; therefore the following information would be given on the first page of the research paper. On the left-hand side, beginning one inch below the top of the page and flush with the left margin, type the following information:

   Your name
   Your instructor's name
   Title of the course
   Date

   Double-space again and center the title of the paper on that line. Double-space between the title and the first line of the text.

6. If your paper does have a cover sheet, it is not necessary to use the attribution given above on the first page. See the Tourette paper example in Appendix A.

7. Do not underline your title, enclose it in quotation marks, or type it in all capital letters. Underline only those words you would underline in the text, such as the title of a book.

8. Put your last name and the page number in the top right-hand corner one-half inch from the top of the page, even on the first page. Number all pages consecutively without using any punctuation and without using the letter *p* before the number. Number the outline page, however, with small Roman numerals—i, ii, and so forth.

   Figure 12.1 shows how the first page of the research paper should be presented using the MLA style. Figure 12.2 shows the following page.

FIGURE 12.1

First page of research paper using MLA style

Wood 1

Ellen Wood

Professor Browning

English 1001

30 October 1999

Tourette Syndrome: A Misunderstood Problem

"I thought maybe I was crazy," Stacy said, "I went through eight doctors. They told me, 'she'll grow out of it.' I knew she wasn't in control, and I told them that. But nobody would listen to me" ("Tourette Syndrome"). This is the account of one mother's quest for answers concerning her daughter's constant clicking sounds, her repetitiveness, and her impulsiveness. Another account is similar. R. David Carpenter said he and his wife "returned from a trip to the Caribbean to find their son Chad had started pushing his upper teeth against his lower teeth with such force as to cause root damage and bleeding." He writes, "He did it in ceremonial fashion, speaking the words, 'one . . . two . . . three,' and concluding loudly saying DONE." That night they "spent in the hospital emergency room only to end up hearing several doctors agree they had never seen anything like it" (par. 4). Jim Eisenreich, outfielder with the Kansas City Royals, says, "I was bounced from one doctor to another and was treated for problems that I didn't have [. . .]. Fortunately, I was eventually diagnosed correctly, and proper treatment now allows me to live a normal life." Tracy Haerle, editor of <u>Children with Tourette Syndrome: A Parents' Guide</u>, notes that she and her husband consulted "an endless stream of physicians" before they were able to get the kind of

FIGURE 12.2

Succeeding pages after the first page

Wood 2

help they needed after their son began showing symptoms at the age of two and a half (vii).

Statements like these could be repeated over and over because of the difficulty in diagnosing Tourette Syndrome or the lack of knowledge on the part of some in the medical field. According to Rick Fowler in The Unwelcome Companion, "Misunderstanding has plagued Tourette Syndrome sufferers since long before the disorder had its name" (17). *This misunderstanding and misdiagnoses of Tourette Syndrome by physicians and psychologists, along with a lack of knowledge by the general public, often causes problems for the individual with Tourette as well as for those associated with him or her.*

Even though Tourette Syndrome was first described by Gilles de la Tourette in 1885, the disorder continues to be misunderstood. Gilles de la Tourette was fascinated by people who had uncontrollable tics—motor tics and vocal tics—and who exhibited obsessive and compulsive behavior disorders. As a result of his studying people with these disorders, the disorder became known as Tourette Syndrome or TS. He noted that these people, despite their odd behaviors, were mentally sound, even though some regarded them as being insane or possessed by demons. However, misunderstanding Tourette Syndrome has plagued TS sufferers since long before the disorder had a name (SerVaas pars. 1, 3). This misunderstanding is true to a great extent because of the lack of control that Tourette sufferers have at times. And, while most people with Tourette have average or above average intelligence and can do anything they want to do, it is the norm for people to look down upon those who are different and regard them as pariahs.

9. Although the *MLA Handbook* does not give specific instructions for a cover page, many instructors prefer one. The following information is usually given and spaced accordingly.

Title of the paper, centered two and one-half inches from the top of the page
Title of the course, centered four inches below the title
The instructor's name, centered two spaces below the course name
Your name, centered two and one-half inches below the instructor's name
Date, centered two spaces below your name

Ask your instructor what he or she would like for you to include. A sample cover page, not to scale, is shown in Figure 12.3.

10. Prepare your Works Cited page.

   a. Center the title "Works Cited" one inch below the top of the page. Double-space between the title and the first entry. Number the pages consecutively with the other pages, as you have done on the previous pages, with your name preceding the page number.

   b. Double-space between the title and the first entry, and double-space both within and between entries.

   c. Begin each entry flush with the left margin; if the entry is more than one line, indent each following line one-half inch from the left margin.

   d. Alphabetize the entries according to the author's or editor's name. If these are not given, alphabetize by the title of the work. (*Note:* Never alphabetize by the words *a, an,* or *the.*)

   e. Remember to use three hyphens, a period, and the title of the book if the entry is by the same author as the previous entry. For example:

```
Orwell, George. Animal Farm. New York: Harcourt,
     1946.
---. 1984. New York: Harcourt, 1949.
```

FIGURE 12.3

Cover page

Tourette Syndrome: A Misunderstood Problem

English 1001

Frances Browning, Instructor

Ellen Wood

30 October 1999

ORDERING THE PAGES OF YOUR PAPER .

Though the order for turning in the pages of your paper may vary from instructor to instructor, the following order is usually followed:

1. Cover page (if required)
2. Outline (if required)
3. Text of your paper
4. Works Cited
5. Blank page

Now that you have finished writing your research paper, you probably feel a sense of accomplishment. This is one of many papers you will write while in school. Having learned the steps for writing a successful research paper, you should experience few difficulties in the future. Although this manual follows the MLA style, which is the format most instructors use, some instructors prefer other styles. If your instructor prefers another style and format, you will only need to adjust the form slightly from MLA style. Be sure to ask your instructor which format he or she prefers. The important point is that you have acquired the essential information about how to write a research paper.

Good luck with this paper and with all of the others you will write!

EXERCISE 1   Preparing the Final Copy

Working in small groups, read through the research papers in Appendices A–C, keeping in mind all that you have learned in this book. If necessary, review any steps that may still seem difficult for you.

Research Paper Using Cause and Effect Order

Tourette Syndrome: A Misunderstood Problem

English 1001
Frances Browning, Instructor

Ellen Wood
30 July 1999

Wood ii

Outline

Thesis: A misunderstanding and misdiagnoses of Tourette Syndrome by physicians and psychologists, along with a lack of knowledge by the general public, often causes problems for the individual with Tourette as well as those associated with the person.

    I.   Introduction
   II.   Definition of Tourette Syndrome
  III.   Misdiagnosing Tourette Syndrome in medical fields
          A.   Symptoms—not based on diagnostic test
          B.   Clinical—based on history and exam
   IV.   Causes of Tourette
          A.   Neurological
          B.   Inherited
          C.   Neurochemical malfunction
    V.   Misunderstanding of Tourette by society
          A.   Of what Tourette is
          B.   Of causes of Tourette
          C.   Of symptoms associated with Tourette
               1.   Ostracized as result of Tourette
               2.   Regarded as demon possessed
          D.   Of effects of Tourette
   VI.   Lack of acceptance of Tourette in business world
          A.   Rigid concept of professional poise
          B.   Respect greater benefit than being liked

Wood iii

VII.   Lack of acceptance in school among peers

     A.   Negative effects

         1. Ryan Farrell

         2. Dr. Larry Burd

         3. Joshua P. Karch

         4. Ten-year-old Mark

     B.   Positive effects

         1. More forgiving

         2. More understanding

         3. More accepting

VIII.   Effect of Tourette on Family

     A.   Parents

     B.   Siblings

         1. Nick Farrell

         2. Julie Hughes

  IX. Conclusion

Wood 1

Tourette Syndrome: A Misunderstood Problem

"I thought maybe I was crazy," Stacy said. "I went through eight doctors. They told me, 'she'll grow out of it.' I knew she wasn't in control, and I told them that. But nobody would listen to me" ("Tourette Syndrome"). This is the account of one mother's quest for answers concerning her daughter's constant clicking sounds, her repetitiveness, and her impulsiveness. Another account is similar. R. David Carpenter said he and his wife "returned from a trip to the Caribbean to find their son Chad had started pushing his upper teeth against his lower teeth with such force as to cause root damage and bleeding." He writes, "He did it in ceremonial fashion, speaking the words, 'one...two...three,' and concluding by loudly saying DONE." That night, they "spent in the hospital emergency room only to end up hearing several doctors agree they had never seen anything like it" (par. 4). Jim Eisenreich, outfielder with the Kansas City Royals, says, "I was bounced from one doctor to another and was treated for problems that I didn't have.[...] Finally, I was eventually diagnosed correctly, and proper treatment now allows me to live a normal life." Tracy Haerle, editor of Children with Tourette Syndrome: A Parents' Guide, notes that she and her husband consulted "an endless stream of physicians" before they were able to get the kind of help they needed after their son began showing symptoms at the age of two and a half (vii).

Wood 2

Statements like these could be repeated over and over because of the difficulty in diagnosing Tourette Syndrome or the lack of knowledge on the part of some in the medical field. According to Rick Fowler in <u>The Unwelcome Companion</u>, "Misunderstanding has plagued Tourette Syndrome sufferers since long before the disorder had its name" (17). *This misunderstanding and misdiagnoses of Tourette Syndrome by physicians and psychologists, along with a lack of knowledge by the general public, often causes problems for the individual with Tourette as well as for those associated with him or her.*

Even though Tourette Syndrome was first described by Gilles de la Tourette in 1885, the disorder continues to be misunderstood. Gilles de la Tourette was fascinated by people who had uncontrollable tics—motor tics and vocal tics—and who exhibited obsessive and compulsive behavior disorders. As a result of his studying people with these disorders, the disorder became known as Tourette Syndrome, or TS. He noted that these people, despite their odd behaviors, were mentally sound, even though some regarded them as being insane or possessed by demons. However, misunderstanding Tourette Syndrome has plagued TS sufferers since long before the disorder had a name (SerVaas pars. 1, 3). This misunderstanding is true to a great extent because of the lack of control that Tourette sufferers have at times. And, while most people with Tourette have average or above average intelligence and can do anything they want to do, it is the norm for people to look down

Wood 3

upon those who are different and regard them as pariahs. Part of the reason is that the public does not understand why those with Tourette act as they do.

Not understanding Tourette is a problem for those in the medical field as well. Doctors have difficulty in determining just what Tourette is and how to diagnose it, whether it should be by symptoms or by a clinical diagnosis. According to Dr. Carl R. Hansen, "Like other 'syndromes,' Tourette Syndrome is so called because it is diagnosed on the basis of the symptoms it produces, not with a specific diagnostic test. Both motor and vocal tics **must be** present for the diagnosis of Tourette Syndrome to be made, but there are also a variety of other symptoms that **may** be present" (Haerle 2). On the other hand, Dr. Ted Chronister, a neurologist in the duPont Hospital for the Children's Division of Neurology, says, "the diagnosis is a clinical one—that is, it's based on the history and what you see in the exam. There are no tests to prove or disprove Tourette" ("Tourette Syndrome"). He points out that a child could have other types of disorders that resemble tics, but that with Tourette tics, other symptoms are present, such as noises and verbalizations. Perhaps the difficulty associated with diagnosing Tourette is one reason that it is often misdiagnosed. Doctors feel that the person with Tourette must have a full-blown case before it is not confused with other disorders. The reason for that assumption is that it is often confounded with other problems, such as attention deficit hyperactivity

Wood 4

disorder (ADHD) or in the past with schizophrenia or obsessive-compulsive disorder or simply a nervous habit.

The latest revision of "The Guide to the Diagnosis and Treatment of Tourette Syndrome" points out that since at least "half of the TS patients have attention deficit and hyperactivity as children, a physician may well be confused" (3). The article also states that "since more physicians are now aware of TS, there is a growing danger of overdiagnosis or overtreatment. Prevailing diagnostic criteria would require that all children with suppressible multiple motor and phonic tics, however minimal, of at least one year, should be diagnosed as having TS" (3). That kind of diagnostic criteria may be valid; however, some facial tics or phonic tics may be caused by allergies or other disorders that may be more prevalent at certain times of the year. A detailed study of an even longer duration may be necessary in order to verify a true diagnosis.

Rick Fowler makes an interesting observation of the difficulties associated with diagnosing Tourette. He notes that it is now known that Tourette is a neurological disorder and not a mental deficiency and that the condition is inherited, caused by a neurochemical malfunction. But he says some well-meaning but misinformed psychiatrists erroneously assume that "symptoms result from a patient's hidden hatred for a parent, suppressed memories of abuse, a desperate need for attention, or some other environmental stressor" (19). It is difficult to understand why such an assumption would be possible, but that only emphasizes the

Wood 5

problem that those with Tourette have in being understood.
At best, diagnosing Tourette, even today, is multifacted
and no simple process. Because of this difficulty, it
should involve an interdisciplinary approach with neurolo-
gists as well as psychiatrists and psychologists included.
Otherwise, too often the result is a misdiagnosis, and the
child suffers because of it, at times becoming depressed
and bewildered because he or she is different and does not
understand why. Ryan said it this way in <u>Ryan: A Mother's
Story of Her Hyperactive/Tourette Syndrome Child</u>, "I HATE
this stupid Tourette Syndrome! I just want to be a REGULAR
kid" (Hughes 96).

In addition to the medical field's difficulty in
diagnosing Tourette, the general public has little
knowledge of the disorder unless someone they know is
afflicted. If people did know more about Tourette and
how it affects the sufferer, it is likely they would be
more accepting of the person with TS. They would develop
an empathy for the person instead of shunning him or her
because of the peculiar symptoms of the disease. They
would realize that Tourette can happen in any family if
the genes are present. It respects no one.

Doctors now know that Tourette Syndrome is much
more common than they once thought, and it is believed
that as many as 100,000 Americans have it. Where once it
was unclear how a person developed Tourette Syndrome,
now it is known that it is inherited as a dominant gene,
with 99 percent of boys with the gene showing symptoms

Wood 6

and 70 percent of girls with the gene displaying symptoms. Usually, the symptoms begin around the age of two
to fifteen, often with the disorder's getting better as
the child grows older, even though the symptoms rarely go
away completely ("A Story of Tourette Syndrome"). Even
though some have severe cases of Tourette that hamper
their activities, most often the person learns to live
with his or her disabilities and, by finding the right
combination of drugs and therapy, is able to function
in society.

The person with TS, as pointed out earlier, may have
motor tics that involve movements of the muscles and vocal
tics that are sounds like throat-clearing, grunting, and
humming. In addition, some have coprolalia or echolalia
(repetition of words). In the WebRing site of the Tourette
Syndrome Web page, Raenna Peiss, states that coprolalia
does not have to be exclusively swear words but may be
socially inappropriate or unacceptable words or phrases.
She adds that "Something about the 'forbiddenness' of it
impels a person with coprolalia to say it, seemingly
against their will" (1). This symptom of Tourette is difficult for most people to understand; they think the person can control what he or she says, but the person who
has Tourette is unable to do so. Some, however, do not say
the unacceptable words or phrases out loud, but in their
minds keep repeating them over and over. They know it is
wrong to say them and therefore exercise great control in
not blurting out what they are thinking.

Wood 7

If people understood the symptoms of Tourette Syndrome—that the person cannot help what he or she is doing or saying—this would help them accept rather than reject the person who has TS. Unfortunately, information is scarce except for those who are affected and for their families. Many well-meaning people do not understand that the person with TS may have odd table manners, spilling food or shaking food off the fork methodically; they may not understand that the person barking like a dog is doing so because of his disorder; they may not understand that the person who has tics has little control over them just as the person who must sneeze has little control over his or her sneezing. Because of their lack of knowledge and resulting lack of understanding, they often denigrate the person with Tourette and cause him or her much psychological harm.

For example, Rick Fowler, who has Tourette, tells of a little boy coming up to him one time when he was having a difficult time with his tics saying, "My little cousin does that. He's been kicked out of school, and his parents have practically disowned him. I'm the only one who will have anything to do with him" (107). Fowler said he recognized that the little boy likely had Tourette Syndrome. His parents and teachers knew so little about the behaviors associated with Tourette they were not able to accept him. Dave Carpenter, whose son has TS, said on his Web page that he received an anonymous packet in the mail that said "Chad was possessed and needed an exorcist to

Wood 8

rid him of the demons." That is the typical opinion of those who are ignorant about the problems of the person with Tourette.

Not only are children the victims of this kind of treatment, but adults who have TS are also mistreated. On Tuesday, 20 July, 1999, AP writer Mike Robinson reported that "Neighbors (in Chicago) of a man with Tourette's Syndrome are trying to force him out of his condominium because his footstomping, hooting, and barking are keeping them awake" (Advocate 9A). Jeffrey Marthon, a 53-year-old lawyer, has been troubled with Tourette Syndrome and its involuntary, abrupt body movements and sounds all of his life. The condominium association where he and his wife live even put a sign on his door asking "Have you no decency?" Marthon is suing the association, saying federal laws protecting the disabled should keep him from being forced out.

These examples may sound far-fetched, but they only emphasize how unknowledgeable people are about this disorder. Somehow, people must be made aware of what Tourette Syndrome is so they can be more supporting of people with Tourette. Dr. Dale Hammerschmidt, associate professor of medicine at the University of Minnesota and also the father of two children with TS, says, "We have to be accepting (of people with TS), rather than making them pariahs [. . .]. We have to make reasonable accommodations for them in school and at work" (MayoClinic, par. 8). Fowler echoes that statement in pointing out the need

Wood 9

for acceptance in the executive world when he says, "It is unfortunate that acceptance does not cross into the business world so easily. Business people frequently have a rigid concept of professional poise, and a person with tics does not fit that image. In the corporate world, being respected is of far greater benefit than being liked" (101). Such comments as these are sad but true.

The problem of not being accepted, then, is a viable one, partially because of the public's lack of awareness of Tourette Syndrome and its symptoms. In order for those with the disorder ever to be accepted so that there will be a change in attitude, the public must be educated about what it is like to have Tourette. When society is knowledgeable about the disorder, there will be less condemnation of the person who is disruptive or who exhibits inappropriate behaviors. Susan Hughes believes that knowledge is the key to acceptance. She says, " [. . .] the majority of people are very understanding, forgiving and sympathetic when approached in a non-confrontive manner" (114). But this will happen only when they are informed.

In addition to society's not accepting and understanding the person with Tourette, children who have TS face problems of not being accepted in school. Fowler says, "Numerous horror stories are told of children with tics who are relentlessly tormented by their classmates, making life at school a living hell" (100). Eleven-year-old Ryan Farrell in his book, God Made Me Special, says:

Wood 10

A lot of the kids were mean and cruel to me because of my Tourette. At the beginning of the year, some of the older kids in the sixth, seventh, and eighth grades called me 'baldie' and said very hurtful things to me. One person said, 'It looks like you have Leukemia with those bald spots.' Another person said, 'You're getting old early because you're losing your hair.' One boy said, 'Your parents must be too poor to get you a hair cut, so they let your brother shave your head.' One boy called me a lizard because of my facial tic. (71)

Dr. Larry Burd, in <u>Children with Tourette Syndrome</u>, writes, "Because of their differences, children with Tourette Syndrome often feel isolated from their class- mates" (194). He said one parent commented that "The other kids call him (her son) 'dummy' and 'troublemaker'" (201). Another said, "The first time anyone in school ever said anything good about my son was in fifth grade, right after the diagnosis of TS. His teacher said, 'He's a neat kid. He's got a lot going for him!' That was the first time I felt my son had a chance to succeed" (202).

Tracey Haerle sees the problem as being one of teach- ers lack of controlling the behavior of children. She says that those in authority need to explain to other children that the child cannot control his or her symptoms and that teasing will not be tolerated (194). That may be easier said than done, but it would be a start in helping the

Wood 11

peers of those with Tourette understand the child with Tourette. It would also help the child with Tourette be able to cope with his disorder.

Joshua P. Karch, on his Web page entitled "An Encounter with Tourette Syndrome," gives a number of responses he received concerning the reactions of children to those who have TS. For example, Andrew Harrison, a student in grade 13 in Canada, says, "I have been made fun of countless times.[. . .] It really bothers me when 'jerks' around the school make fun of my tics and give me strange looks" (7). He then adds, "I'm ignoring the 'jerks' who give me a hard time. I also have noticed the 'jerks' seem to be many of the less mature people around the school" (8). And ten-year-old Mark who gets second looks from people because of his twitches, shrugs, and shoulder jerks, says, "One time some kid asked me why I was moving like that. Before I could answer, another kid said, 'Because he's weird.'" (KidsHealth 1). But Mark wasn't weird; he just had Tourette. Children like Mark may seem different, but they want to be treated like anyone else. They can do anything other children can do; they just have a disorder that makes them act differently; they're still human beings who want to be accepted for who and what they are, not for their tics.

Though having Tourette is difficult, sometimes positive things do happen, and one of the positive things that happens to many of the children is they learn how to forgive. As Ryan Farrell says, "I know that God made me

Wood 12

special because I was able to forgive [. . .]. One thing that my Tourette has taught me is how to forgive; I am so used to forgiving people for making fun of me" (77). Andrew Harrison in Joshua Karch's home page echoes that sentiment by saying, "Because you have Tourette's, you can become easily a more understanding person because you can relate to others' problems. You, therefore, become a more understanding person, and those who laugh at you only end up looking like uncaring, uneducated 'jerks'" (7). Tourette, then, while incapacitating and debilitating, does not have to have only downsides. The person with TS often is more compassionate and more accepting of others and more understanding of those who have limitations.

The child with Tourette, however, while often able to compensate to some degree for the way he is treated, is not the only person affected. Many times, the family and siblings feel at a loss in knowing how and what to do with the person who has TS. They find themselves venting their frustrations on the one afflicted, which only compounds the problem for the child. He or she feels rejected by those who should love him or her most. But the family is not entirely to blame; they just do not know any better. They do not know how to handle a person who is out of control. They may feel that the child could behave differently if he or she so chose, not realizing that he or she can do little to control his or her behavior. It is the disorder that causes the temper tantrums and obnoxious behavior.

Wood 13

Because of having Tourette himself, Fowler understands the problem from the vantage point of one with the
disorder. He says, "Some [those with TS] have no love and
support from the people around them. They must face both
the torturous symptoms of their illness and the damaging
curse of being rejected by those nearest to them" (8).
That is especially devastating to the child with Tourette.
Instead of being accepted and loved for who he or she is,
the child is rejected for a disorder over which he or she
has no control. The same rejection is often experienced by
parents of the child with Tourette as Susan Hughes, who
has a son with Tourette, explains. She points out that
"Parents of children with Tourette Syndrome deserve our
compassion and understanding, but many times instead of
sympathy or compassion, they receive criticism and harsh
judgments from people who are not aware of the circumstances they face" (113). This attitude is shown when the
TS child exhibits behavior that is unacceptable, such as
with coprolalia or even echolalia. Instead of trying to
understand what causes the child to do the things he or
she does and supporting the parents who are doing their
best to cope with the problem, people with this response
do what comes naturally—criticize.

To illustrate the frustration that some parents feel,
Haerle in her Parents' Guide, says one neighbor suggested
the parent of a child with Tourette get a life and quit
paying too much attention to her daughter who had TS. She
accused her of being underinvolved and neglectful, while

Wood 14

others accused her of being overinvolved and smothering
(137). Another parent's therapist said, "Oh, 'impulsiveness.' That's a convenient excuse people use to continue
lazy parenting" (136). It is clear the people who made
these statements were not educated about the nature of
Tourette Syndrome or they would have been more understanding and compassionate.

While Tourette is a problem for the person with the
disorder, it is a problem for the whole family as well. As
Susan Hughes says, "Tourette Syndrome does not just affect
the patient; it affects the whole family, and the whole
family must learn to adjust to the circumstances on an
individual basis" (116). It often causes parents to
divorce because they simply cannot handle the stress of
not knowing what is in store for them. Others adopt the
attitude that we are in it "for better or worse," as the
marriage vows say, and their marriage becomes stronger. It
would be wrong, though, to say that other family members
are not affected. For example, Nick, Ryan Farrell's little
brother says:

> Sometimes I feel mad at my family because Ryan gets
> so much attention. I know my family loves me, but I
> still get mad at Ryan's Tourette because if he didn't
> have it, he wouldn't get the attention of our mom and
> dad. I also get mad at Ryan's Tourette because some-
> times he isn't very nice to me. He says he's sorry
> when he's mean to me, and most of the time I forgive

Wood 15

him. I love my brother, even though it's hard, so I put up with his Tourette. (107)

Susan Hughes, in her book about her son, also named Ryan, says she regrets that she has not been able to give the amount of quality time to her daughter Julie since she has to spend as much time with Ryan. She points out, however, that "Despite the abuse and turmoil she has endured, Julie always manages to give Ryan another chance and is very protective of him when others criticize him" (100). This kind of devotion does not always exist between siblings. More often, the extra attention that has to be paid to the afflicted child causes sibling rivalry, and tension increases for the whole family. Dr. Carl Hansen gives good advice in this respect. He advises parents to treat their other children not just as siblings of their child with Tourette Syndrome, but to appreciate them for who they are. He adds that if too much time is spent with the child who has TS, other siblings may feel neglected and jealous and unloved, which may cause them to misbehave (Haerle 125, 126). Tourette, then, can easily disrupt the family because of the time spent with the TS child and because of the difficulty in knowing what to do. Other children suffer as well in having to adjust to a situation that often demands more give-and-take than they can handle. This is just one more problem associated with Tourette.

It is easy to see, then, that Tourette Syndrome has many negative effects. It too often begins with a misdiagnosis by those in the medical field because of their lack of understanding of the nature of Tourette. It is compounded by the lack of knowledge and acceptance by people in general. The key, therefore, to an understanding and acceptance of Tourette is education—first by physicians and psychiatrists, next by the general public and finally within the child's own family. When more people know about Tourette and understand why those with the disorder act as they do, half the battle of acceptance will be won. In the meantime, it is important to remember that kids with Tourette are no different from other kids. Tics don't make them different inside. "In fact, some famous people who have Tourette Syndrome do some pretty cool stuff—like Philadelphia Phillies outfielder Jim Eisenreich [. . .], Denver Nuggets guard Mahmoud Abdul Rauf, and the real-life brother of Neve Campbell, an actress on the TV show Party of Five (KidsHealth 3). In addition, Fowler states that "Investigators have turned up evidence that Peter the Great and Napoleon Bonaparte, two of history's greatest military leaders, probably suffered from TS" (113). He adds that Mozart, the great composer, and Dr. Samuel Johnson, the British lexicographer and writer thought to be "the greatest man of his time," both were believed to have TS (14). It is clear, then, from these examples that, while Tourette may have been a limitation for them to overcome, those with Tourette can do anything they want to do. They just have to try a little harder.

Wood 17

Works Cited

Bruun, Ruth Dowling, et al. "Guide to the Diagnosis and
    Treatment of Tourette Syndrome." Internet Mental
    Health 1997. 7 July 1999
    <http://mentalhealth.com/book/p40-gtor.html>.

Carpenter, R. David. Home page. 13 July 1999
    <http://www.citynet.net/personal/chad/index1.html>.

Eisenreich, Jim. Foreword. Children with Tourette
    Syndrome: A Parents' Guide. Ed. Tracy Haerle.
    Rockville: Woodbine, 1992.

Farrell, Ryan C. God Made Me Special. Westerville:
    Raspberry, 1997.

Fowler, Rick. The Unwelcome Companion: An Insider's View
    of Tourette Syndrome. Cashiers: Silver Run, 1996.

Haerle, Tracy, ed. Children with Tourette Syndrome: A
    Parents' Guide. Rockville: Woodbine, 1992.

Hughes, Susan. Ryan: A Mother's Story of Her
    Hyperactive/Tourette Syndrome Child. Duarte: Hope,
    1995.

Karch, Joshua P. "An Encounter with Tourette's
    Syndrome." Home page. 13 July 1999
    <http://cec.wustl.edu/~jpk1/tourettes.html>.

Peiss, Raenna. "The Facts about Tourette Syndrome." The
    Tourette Syndrome Chapter WebRing site. Tripod. 13
    July 1999 <http://members.tripod.com/tourette13>.

Robinson, Mike. "Man Who Has Tourette's Fights Eviction
    Effort," The Advocate [Baton Rouge] 20 July 1999: 9A.

Wood 18

SerVaas, Cory. "I have Tourette Syndrome. I don't know
    much about it. Is it a disability? (Ask Dr. Cory)."
    <u>Children's Digest</u> (July-August 1998). <u>InfoTrac</u>.
    2 June 1999 <http://tsa.mgh.harvard.edu>.
"A Story of Tourette Syndrome." <u>KidsHealth.Org For Kids</u>.
    America Online. 13 July 1999
    <http://kidshealth.org/kid/normal/k-tourette.html>.
"Tourette Syndrome: A Mother's Quest for Answers."
    <u>KidsHealth.Org For Parents</u>. America Online. 14 July
    1999
    <http://kidshealth.org/parent/behavior/tourette.html>.
"Tourette's Syndrome: Startling Behaviors That Can Be
    Disconcerting." <u>MayoClinicHealthOasis</u>.3 March 1997.
    America Online. 14 July 1999
    <http://www/mayohealth.org/mayo/9703/htm/tourette.htm>.

Research Paper Using Comparison/ Contrast Order

Tyson 1

Mona Lisa Tyson

Nell W. Meriwether, Instructor

English IV

10 February 1996

An Analysis of the Heath in Selected Works

Each geographical region around the world, whether small or large, country or continent, has a portion of land within its boundaries that overpowers and dominates all others. Examples are the dry deserts of Africa, the swamplands of Louisiana, and the extreme conditions of Siberia in Russia. These vast and distinctive areas possess individual characteristics that enable each to overwhelm its inhabitants, surrounding lands, and oftentimes nature itself. These examples give an idea of the role that the heath plays in <u>Wuthering Heights</u>, <u>King Lear</u>, and <u>The Return of the Native</u>.

Harold Bloom quotes Thomas Hardy in referring to the heath in <u>The Return of the Native</u>, saying:

> The face of the heath by its mere complexion added half an hour to evening; it could in like manner retard the dawn, sudden noon, anticipate the frowning of storms scarcely generated, and intensify the opacity of a moonless midnight to a cause of shaking and dread. (<u>Views</u> 22)

Tyson 2

According to Thomas Hardy, the heath is a barren
land, occupying space as far as the eye can see, whose
inhabitants look out upon it in the darkest hours of night
feeling trapped, never to escape, wondering about the
world beyond (56).

Not only Hardy, but also Emily Brontë and William
Shakespeare share similar views about the heath. Even
though their styles and interpretations differ slightly,
it is evident through these selected works that Hardy,
Brontë, and Shakespeare share the same feeling. They
emphasize the effect the heath has on the lives of their
characters by directly associating it with the characters
and surrounding conditions.

Admittedly, an opposite point of view can be supported showing that Brontë, Shakespeare, and Hardy do not
use the heath symbolically nor do they directly relate it
to the characters and their daily situations. This opinion
can indeed be argued; however, there is more substantial
evidence and indication in their works to convincingly
show the effective use of the heath.

Wuthering Heights, a novel written by Emily Brontë,
is a passionate story of unkindled love, hatred, strife,
and revenge. What seems to be an endless conflict is basically centered around the Earnshaws and the Lintons, two
families who are proprietors of separate plots of land,
and Heathcliff, an orphan whose character further
increases the intensity of the conflict. Wuthering Heights

Tyson 3

and Thrushcross Grange are the plots of land previously mentioned, which are significantly divided by the heath. This open tract of wasteland, which Brontë occasionally refers to as the moors, presents itself not only as a natural obstacle to those who travel through it, but also as a way of looking at Heathcliff's inner being.

The heath definitely symbolizes barrenness and wildness in <u>Wuthering Heights</u>. Tom Winnifrith agrees that the heath is like a harsh landscape that is like barren moors (60). This stretch of "untamed" land is portrayed as a mighty hindrance and burden to those who live and travel upon it. In <u>Wuthering Heights</u>, Mr. Lockwood says, "Yesterday afternoon set in misty and cold, I had half a mind to spend it by the fire, instead of wading through the heath and mud to Wuthering Heights" (6). This obviously shows that the heath is not a desirable place to be nor to pass through due to unfavorable conditions.

The characters of <u>Wuthering Heights</u> are essential elements when considering the heath and its dominant characteristics. The heath causes an inevitable effect on the characters, because there is such a close relationship between them. The inhabitants of such an overbearing land as the heath are not able to avoid some kind of physical or mental contact with it. In the novel, Healthcliff is more closely related to the heath than any other character. Winnifrith states, "[. . .] <u>Wuthering Heights</u> is set in a wild landscape, and it is part of Heathcliff's attraction that he is associated with the landscape and with Wuthering

Tyson 4

Heights" (65). Heathcliff has a certain sense of oneness with the heath. Even his name is linked to the heath. In her introduction to the second edition of Wuthering Heights, Brontë gives a shocking hint concerning the origins of Heathcliff's name. Winnifrith quotes her as saying:

> Most readers will think of a heath as an arid waste as in King Lear, and there are plenty of barren wastes on the moors near Wuthering Heights and in Heathcliff's heart. But there is also a small flower named a heath, and it is to this that links the mighty and rugged cliff that stands for Wuthering Heights. (7)

Critics have always had something to say about Wuthering Heights, whether good or bad. The following critical reviews by Hobart, Garrod, and Schorer are accredited to Nineteenth-Century Literary Criticism and show the critics' impression of the heath. Hobart acknowledges Wuthering Heights as "[. . .] a picture of fierce and strong human nature, utterly untutored and untamed, left to run wild in the gloomy loneliness of a farm on the northern moors" (67).

Garrod comments: "Out of the defects, Wuthering Heights is redeemed, first by its strong instinct for a living scene nowhere else, perhaps save in Lear, and the scene and the actors to the same degree a single tragical effect" (78). Garrod continues with, "The very title 'Wuthering Heights' is a stroke of inspiration. Heathcliff

Tyson 5

has just one name, no other, as though he were a piece of the moorland—'an arid wilderness' [. . .]" (78).

Finally, Mark Schorer remarks in the same criticism, "Human conditions are like the activities of the land-scape; faces, too, are like landscapes in <u>Wuthering Heights</u>" (91). These critics, in expounding upon the rela-tionship between the heath and the characters of the novel, show the strong impact of the heath upon the tragic events that occur.

Another literary work already alluded to that stresses the effect of the heath on the characters is <u>King Lear</u>, one of Shakespeare's greatest plays. It is a power-ful tragedy about an aged king who decides to divide his kingdom among his three daughters, giving the largest share to the one who can prove she loves him most. The youngest and favorite daughter refuses her father's request because she can see the deceit in her two older sisters in their professions of love. King Lear is out-raged, and he banishes her from his kingdom, giving the land to the two remaining daughters. Soon after, Lear's daughters become ungrateful and strip him of everything he owns, which then leads to the king's insanity. When King Lear goes out on the heath amidst a terrible storm, he is at a breaking point in his life. It is at the climax of the story that he realizes the foolishness of his actions. Later he dies of a broken heart.

In <u>King Lear</u>, the heath again symbolizes an "arid" and desolate land and is often compared with the heath in

Tyson 6

<u>Wuthering Heights</u>, but there is an underlying purpose in Shakespeare's heath. Not only is it the place where he pours his heart out as he realizes the futility of his actions, but it is also a comforter to Lear as he confesses his mistakes. Accompanied by his Fool in the storm, he gains compassion and understanding from his surroundings even though he is weakened and at the point of insanity.

In <u>Essentials of English Literature</u>, Bernard Grebanier states, "The elements are now raging. Amidst sheets of lightning, volleys of thunder, and cascades of rain, Lear wanders on the heath in the company of his Fool" (120). Sylvia Goulding affirms that what happened upon the heath during that fierce storm was a turning point in King Lear's life; his insanity and rage cause him to go out in such a storm and relieve his mind of his burdens (19).

In Act Three, Scene Four, Lear is truly at his lowest level in life. It is at this moment on the heath that he reaches his catharsis, meaning that the foolishness of his actions are revealed to him. Russell Fraser, in the introduction to <u>The Tragedy of King Lear</u>, writes, "It is also on the heath that Lear is made pregnant to pity" (23). This is an indication of the severity of his sorrow and distress. It is clear then that King Lear reaches the climax of his desperate situation on the heath with Edgar and his Fool (Foster 1164). Even though the luxuries of kingship are taken from him, it is on the heath that Lear

Tyson 7

touches his true inner self and the real experiences of
the people and the world around him he could not acquire
among the glory and power of being a king.

Another literary work, The Return of the Native by
Thomas Hardy, also uses the heath in such proportions that
it achieves nearly anthropomorphic dimensions, the first
chapter's being devoted almost entirely to a discussion of
the heath. The two opposing forces in the novel are Egdon
Heath, a vast tract of wasteland, and Eustacia Vye, a
young woman struggling against the heath in vain. All
other actions in the story seem to be concentrated upon
these two forces.

The plot basically consists of a small group of
people who are trying to solve major conflicts among themselves but are not too successful, because they are faced
with the presence and dominating personality of the heath
each day of their lives. Egdon Heath presents itself as a
no-way-out situation. Nothing leaves the realms of Egdon
Heath.

Thomas Hardy was born almost on Egdon Heath—which he
made immortal—in Dorset, near Dorchester. Egdon Heath is a
justifiable portrayal of his homeland at Higher
Bockhampton on the edge of Puddleton Heath. Hardy's close
association with the heath explains why Egdon Heath is
such a dominating force in the novel.

Though Hardy wrote a number of novels, The Return of
the Native is the only one that precisely links the land

Tyson 8

with the plot throughout the entire book. Woodcock, in
the introduction to <u>The Return of the Native</u>, states:

> When Hardy describes the face of the Heath, with its
> seasonal moods and diurnal changes, [. . .] he is
> working from memory, and it is not surprising that on
> these occasions he slips into the manner of a rural
> essayist rather than a writer of fiction. (15)

Hardy's experience with the heath as a child gives him a
cutting edge when he writes his novels.

Hardy describes the heath as a vast stretch of wild
land with no boundaries. It is like the floor of a tent
made up of an empty stretch of clouds that block the sky
(53). This allows the mind to form a mental picture of how
massive and coarse the heath really is. It is illustrated
as a living landscape that humans must be bound to if they
are to survive. Those who lack in the kind of determination to survive tend to struggle with the land, which in
the end leads to failure in life or death. The heath is an
"untamable" stretch of land that regards civilization as
its enemy, rejects vegetation on its soil, and wears the
natural and unchanged look as it did when it was first
formed (56). Hardy further adds, "The sea changed, the
fields changed, the rivers, the villages, and the people
changed, yet Egdon remained" (56). This gives a definite
account of the heath's uniform structure and appearance

Tyson 9

throughout time. Hardy explains an overall atmosphere in view of the heath when he says:

It could be best felt when it could not clearly be seen, its complete effect and explanation lying in this and the succeeding hours before the next dawn. Then, and only then, did it tell its true tale. (53)

In The Return of the Native, Egdon Heath represents more than just the root of the inhabitants' sufferings, though it is thought to be the basis of their troubles. Wester says, "The Heath acts as more than the setting; it assumes a part of a major character" (1894), while Gregor feels that Egdon Heath can be introduced as the chief character of the novel (69). Gregor argues that though Hardy explains the role distinction of the heath between "land" and "character" in the beginning chapters of the novel, there is still difficulty in understanding how the heath makes such a transition. He declares: "The ruling passions of the protagonists in The Return of the Native, and the awesome powers of the Heath need to be treated as forces of like nature—the Heath manifesting the same impulses as do the fictional characters" (95). This interpretation by Gregor expounds on the fact that Egdon Heath is a major character in the novel.

The heath has another significant role. It is the place where Mrs. Yeobright, Eustacia, and Wildeve die.

Tyson 10

These deaths confirm the belief that the heath is a firm enemy, and those who fight against it will eventually die.

The influences of Egdon Heath are gripping and long lasting. Six main characters in The Return of the Native acquire a characteristic from the heath. Clym, Mrs. Yeobright, and Diggory Venn share its appearance of separateness. A quality of stamina is seen in Clym, Thomasin, and Venn. Finally, Eustacia and Wildeve share beginning liveliness and fairness to others (Bloom Views 55). Woodcock writes, "It [the novel] is set in Egdon Heath whose lowering 'titanic' presence dominates the men and women who live on it . . ." (Blurb, Return). These statements indicate that Egdon Heath controlled the lives of the inhabitants and reveal the influential power of such a barren wasteland.

Out on the heath, Mrs. Yeobright notices Clym, her son, at work and describes his appearance as being "not more distinguishable from the scene around him than the green caterpillar from the leaf it feeds on" (Bloom Interpretations 81). Her statement suggests that the inhabitants of the heath blend with one another.Basically, the identifiable features and characteristics of a person are consumed by the heath, and his individuality is drained and absorbed into the land. Later she says, "He [Clym] appeared as a mere parasite of the Heath [. . .] having no knowledge of anything in the world but fern, furze, heath, liches, and moss" (Bloom Interpretations 81). This establishes a summary of how the heath constantly preys upon the people

Tyson 11

and how there is not an escape from the overwhelming and
unseen boundaries that confine the inhabitants of their
fate.

Opinions, however, are usually divided when it comes
to critiquing The Return of the Native regarding the
heath. Some critics have a difficult time figuring out
which point to emphasize or which side to take; however,
reviews by Gregor, Wester, Scott-James, and Welton are
concise and straight to the point. According to Gregor:

When the reader comes to reflect upon his experience
of reading The Return of the Native, he is left, I
think, with the distinct impression that the dramatic
life of the novel is vividly present in the first
book, which is dominated by Egdon Heath [. . .]. (69)

Wester points out in her criticism that "the Heath becomes
a symbol of permanence" (1984). Scott-James notes:

Hardy's magnificient beginning of The Return of the
Native, showing in the description of Egdon Heath
what sort of place it is in which the persons are to
suffer, creates an impression of nature more somber
than we have had before, indeed a nature that appears
to share the suffering of man. (7)

Finally, Welton, in Great Writers of the English
Language, writes, "The wilderness of Egdon Heath [. . .]

Tyson 12

provides a somber, brooding backdrop for the passionate love stories played out in this gripping tale" (74). She concludes, "The monotonous way of life for the people of the Heath and the slow pace at which the novel progresses carries with it a sense of timelessness and inevitability (74). It is clear, then, from critics as well as from simply reading the novel, that the heath is a viable force in the lives of the characters and in what happens to them.

It is also obvious, after extensive research, that the characters and their circumstances are symbolically and directly affected by the heath in Wuthering Heights, King Lear, and The Return of the Native. The heath proves itself to be an invincible foe against anyone or anything that steps into its mighty walls. It is even personified as possessing human qualities, achieving anthropomorphic proportions. Bloom best describes the heath in all three works as being "slighted, enduring, obscure, obsolete, and superseded by none. (Interpretations 122). After close analysis, it is evident that the heath, that massive stretch of wild and desolate land, possesses power and strength beyond the imagination.

Tyson 13

Works Cited

Abbey, Cherie D., and Janet Mullane, eds. <u>Nineteenth-</u>
    <u>Century Literary Criticism</u>. Vol. 16. Detroit: Gale,
    1987.

Bloom, Harold, ed. <u>Modern Critical Views: Thomas Hardy</u>.
    New York: Chelsea, 1987.

---. <u>Modern Critical Interpretations: Thomas Hardy's</u>
    Return of the Native. New York: Chelsea, 1987.

Brontë, Emily. <u>Wuthering Heights</u>. New York: Bantam, 1981.

Foster, Edward E. "King Lear." <u>1300 Critical Evaluations</u>
    <u>of Selected Novels</u>. Ed. Frank N. Magill. Vol 2.
    Englewood Cliffs: Salem, 1978. 1164.

Fraser, Russell. Introduction. <u>The Tragedy of King Lear</u>.
    By William Shakespeare. New York: Penguin, 1987.

Goulding, Sylvia and Jude Welton, eds. <u>Great Writers of</u>
    <u>the English Language</u>. New York: Marshall Cavendish,
    1989.

Grebanier, Bernard D. N., <u>Essentials of English</u>
    <u>Literature</u>. Vol. 1. New York: Barron's, 1959.

Gregor, Ian. "Landscapes with Figures." <u>Modern Critical</u>
    <u>Interpretations: Thomas Hardy's</u> Return of the
    Native." New York: Chelsea, 1987.

Hardy, Thomas. <u>The Return of the Native</u>. New York:
    Penguin, 1978.

Scott-James, R. A. "Thomas Hardy: The Novels and the
    Dynasts." <u>British Writers</u>. Ed. Ian Scott-Kilbert.
    Vol. 6. New York: Scribner's, 1983.

Tyson 14

Shakespeare, William. <u>The Tragedy of King Lear</u>. New York:
    Penguin, 1987.

Wester, Janet. "The Return of the Native." <u>1300 Critical
    Evaluations of Selected Novels and Plays</u>. Ed. Frank
    N. Magill. Vol. 3. Englewood Cliffs: Salem, 1978.
    1894.

Winnifrith, Tom. "Emily Brontë." <u>Dictionary of Literary
    Biography</u>. Eds. Ira B. Nadel and William E. Fredeman.
    Vol. 21. Detroit: Gale, 1983.

Woodcock, George. Introduction. <u>The Return of the Native</u>.
    By Thomas Hardy. New York: Penguin, 1978.

APPENDIX
C

Research Paper Using Particular to General Order and Endnotes

OTHER FORMS OF REFERENCING

For many years, students were advised to use a form of referencing in which the Latin terms *ibid.*, *op. cit.*, and *loc. cit.* were used for subsequent references after the first reference was made. The *MLA Handbook* discourages their use, simply advising that these abbreviations are not recommended.

Another form of referencing, called *documenting notes*, is often used instead of parenthetical notation. With this form of referencing, you will need a list of the works cited or a bibliography to be included at the end of your paper. This is in addition to the endnote page that lists the references you used in your paper. On this page, you will list the works that were cited in your paper according to the same format given in Step 10.

Note Numbers

With note references, the notes are numbered consecutively, with an abbreviated form used for the second referencing. The reader then finds the source at the end of the paper instead of throughout the paper. Because this form is also widely used, directions for its use are included in this section. See the sample paper that follows for examples.

1. Number the references consecutively throughout the paper.
2. Raise the number slightly above the line, after the punctuation.
3. Place the number after the sentence or quoted material.

Footnotes

Occasionally, your instructor may prefer footnotes. The difference between footnotes and endnotes is simply that footnotes occur at the bottom of the page, beginning four lines (two double spaces) below the text. Single-space footnotes, but double-space between them. They are in consecutive order, as are endnotes, and the number is raised slightly above the entry. Otherwise, the format is the same as for endnotes.

Form for the Endnotes Page

1. The Endnotes page immediately follows the rest of the research paper, with the title "Notes" centered one inch from the top of the page.
2. Indent five spaces, set the reference number slightly above the line, and begin the first line of the entry.
3. Subsequent lines of the entry are flush to the left margin.
4. Begin with the author's or editor's names, first name first, followed by a comma.
5. The title of the work follows the name, with no punctuation after it.
6. Next include the publication information in parentheses, with no punctuation following it.
7. The page number appears last, followed by a period.

Sample Entries

Book by one author

¹Peter L. Thorslev, Jr., <u>The Byronic Hero</u> (U.S.A.: Lund, 1962) 111.

Book by two or more authors (or editors)

²Sylvia Goulding and Jude Welton, eds., <u>Great Writers of the English Language</u> (New York: Marshall Cavendish, 1989) 74.

Work in an Anthology

³William Wordsworth, "The World Is Too Much with Us," <u>World Literature</u> (Dallas: Harcourt, 1993) 1004.

An Article in a Reference Book

⁴"English Literature," <u>Encyclopedia Britannica</u>, 1988 ed.

A Multivolume Work

⁵Malcolm Kelsall, "George Gordon, Lord Byron, <u>Cain</u>," <u>British Writers</u>, ed. Ian Scott-Kilbert, vol. 4 (New York: Scribner's, 1981) 181.

An Article in a Magazine

⁶Eugene Linden, "Urban Gorillas," <u>Time</u> 28 June 1999: 50.

An Article in an Online Periodical

⁷Cory SerVaas, "I have Tourette syndrome. I don't know much about it. Is it a disability? (Ask Dr. Cory)," <u>Children's Digest</u> (July-August 1998). InfoTrac. 2 June 1999 <http://tsa.mgh.harvard.edu/>.

Work from an Online Service

    [8]"Tourette Syndrome: A Mother's Quest for Answers."
    KidsHealth.org For Parents, America Online, 14 July 1999
    <http://www.kidshealth.org/parent/behavior/tourette.html>.

Subsequent References

After documenting the work the first time, use a shortened form in subsequent notes; however, as with parenthetical notations, include enough information to identify the work. Usually, the author's last name followed by the relevant page number(s) is adequate. If two or more works are by the same author, you will need to cite the author's last name and a shortened form for the title.

Bibliography Page or Works Cited Page

This page, as already noted, is different from the Endnotes page. While it contains essentially the same information as the Endnotes page, the format is different. With footnotes, this page is an absolute necessity because it lists the referenced works in alphabetical order rather than in the order in which they were used.

1. This page comes after the Endnotes page.
2. All entries appear in alphabetical order.
3. The author or editor's last name appears first, then first name, with a period following it. This helps you alphabetize the entries.
4. The title of the work comes next, followed by a period.
5. The publication data (not in parentheses), followed by a period, appears after the title.
6. Page numbers are not included unless you are citing a periodical.
7. Entries begin at the left-hand margin with the second and third lines indented five spaces (or one-half inch). All entries are double-spaced.

In Step 10, Compiling the Works Cited Page, information was given concerning the different sources you might use. The information is essentially the same for the Bibliography page. Use the guidelines from Step 10 to help you cite your sources.

Milton's Satan and the Byronic Hero

English IV

Nell W. Meriwether, Instructor

Sara Elizabeth Popham

5 December 1995

Popham ii

Outline

Purpose: To show that Byron's heroes are based on Milton's Satan because Byron was attempting to clearly restate the beliefs that he felt Milton said only vaguely in <u>Paradise Lost</u>.

Introduction

   I. Con viewpoint

      A. Byron's personal beliefs

      B. Byron's character's belief

  II. Similarities in Byron's Lucifer and Milton's Satan

      A. Ways they are similar

      B. Byron's words versus Byron's true feelings

 III. Speeches

      A. <u>Paradise Lost</u>

      B. <u>Cain</u>

  IV. Popular beliefs

      A. <u>Paradise Lost</u>

      B. Romantic Era

   V. Outcasts of society

      A. <u>Paradise Lost</u>

      B. <u>Childe Harold</u>

      C. <u>Cain</u>

  VI. Haunted heroes (past wrongs)

      A. <u>Paradise Lost</u>

      B. <u>Cain</u>

      C. <u>Manfred</u>

Popham iii

VII. Protest establishment

     A. <u>Paradise Lost</u>

     B. Anne Radcliffe

     C. <u>Cain</u>

     D. <u>Childe Harold</u>

     E. Don Juan

VIII. Conclusion

Popham 1

Milton's Satan and the Byronic Hero

John Milton wrote <u>Paradise Lost</u> during a time in which strict Puritanism and severe religious practices were the law in England. Absolute reverence and fear of God were the most prized virtues. Milton, a Puritan, wrote an epic that was a retelling of the biblical story of man's expulsion from the paradise of Eden. Through the ages, however, people have seen Milton's <u>Paradise Lost</u> in a new and different light. For many reasons, some believe that it was Satan, and not God or man, that Milton intended to be the hero of <u>Paradise Lost</u>.

Milton never states that Satan is a hero; in fact, he denounces Satan at every available opportunity in his work. However, there are certain aspects of the story that tell a different side. For instance, while God seems to play a small role, Satan is given long speeches, and his statements are made up of the strongest, most effective language. No point he makes is ever disproved. Also, Satan seems to support the Puritan cause, while God seems to represent the tyrant king who has no real right to rule. Satan is the one who opposes God, claiming in dramatic, reasonable tones why he should be deposed. Shelley, in his "Defense of Poetry," says that Satan is actually more humane than God because when God punishes Adam, it seems to be out of malicious sadism rather than out of any real wish to teach Adam repentance.[1]

Popham 2

In fact, it is the Romantic interpretation of Milton's Satan by poets like Shelley, Coleridge, and Blake that really seem to make a hero out of Satan.[2] "Nothing can exceed the energy and magnificence of the character of Satan as expressed in Paradise Lost," Shelley says.[3] Blake says that Milton is "of the devil's party without knowing it," suggesting that Milton intends for Satan to be his hero, and even puts part of himself into his character.[4] Shelley even uses Milton's Satan as a basis for his own hero. Prometheus, in "Prometheus Unbound," says, "The only imaginary being resembling in any degree Prometheus is Satan."[5]

George Gordon, Lord Byron, is another Romantic poet who is said to have "slapped British prudery in the face."[6] His poems are full of revolutionary heroes and protests against convention and conservatives. Byron despises poems that praise "sensibility and sympathy," and he declares "allegiance" to Milton.[7] In many ways his heroes closely resemble Milton's Satan and support his values. While Milton is writing for Puritans and has to defend God and make Him triumphant, Byron does not have to, something that must have pleased him—and perhaps Shelley and Blake as well. He sees this character of Romantic rebellions possessing "courage never to submit or yield"[8] and never allows him to be defeated in his own stories. He takes up Milton's cause in a way that Milton never could. Byron bases his heroes on Milton's Satan because he is trying to restate clearly the beliefs that he thinks Milton has said only vaguely in Paradise Lost.

Popham 3

Contrarily, some argue that Byron was merely stating the beliefs of any Romantic poet. Thorslev in <u>The Byronic Hero</u> says, "The 'aggressive and inventive' heroes are the basis for Romantic self-reliance."[9] Blake praises "the imaginative artist as the true hero."[10] Others claim that Byron did not believe as his characters did. Byron himself states this of his characters Lucifer and Cain in <u>Cain</u>. He claims that he does not agree with them, that he is merely giving them the appropriate attitudes for their parts. However, there are many points to challenge this.

To see the influences of Milton and Byron, the similarities between Milton's Satan and Byron's Lucifer must be examined. Both of them have powerful and convincing speeches condemning God for his unfair practices. They do so with patient reason and quite plausible arguments. When asked by one of the fallen angels if he would return to Heaven if God decided to forgive him, Milton's Satan replies that "It is better to reign in Hell, than serve in Heaven."[11] When confronted with the charge that he brings evil to the world, Byron's Lucifer says:

> Evil and good are things in their own essence,
> And not made good or evil by the Giver;
> But if He gives you good—so call him;
> If evil springs from him, do not name it mine.[12]

In these examples, not only the distinct similarities between the two characters are seen, but also the sense

Popham 4

represented by both. Byron says he does not believe as his characters believe, but in no place in the story does Byron ever disprove, or even dispute, their point of view. God appears to be exactly what Lucifer implies he is—"a gloomy tyrant who denies man knowledge and imposes submission by ignorance."[13] The "good" people in the story are kind to each other, but they are totally submissive to God and lack any character or individuality. When confronted by God for killing his brother, Cain claims that he himself is nothing more than "such as thou [God] madst him; and seeks nothing/Which must be won by kneeling [. . .]."[14] This shows how much more interesting and complex a character Cain is than any of his "good" family. Byron seems only to demonstrate Cain's bravery and independence in daring to challenge God and to desire nothing that can be acquired only by being subservient. For all that Byron denies, he shares his heroes' beliefs in <u>Cain</u>, if not stated, at least unconsciously.

Certainly, this brings up one of the major similarities between the heroes of Byron and Milton's Satan. Even while Byron denies his allegiance to them, Satan and the Byronic heroes are constantly giving convincing, powerful speeches that probe the rightness of their stand beyond doubt, and no event in the story seems to disprove what they say. Blake says in his <u>Milton</u> that Milton's Spectre is Satan and that "Milton acknowledges the validity of Reason, his Spectre. Once Milton is united with his Spectre, he can preach effectively to the public."[15] Steadman, in <u>Milton and</u>

Popham 5

the Paradoxes of Renaissance Heroism, states that "Milton's allegations clash with his demonstrations."[16] And, so it appears, do Byron's. One prime example of the way in which Byron's heroes and Milton's Satan seem to get the reader on the side of their characters is the manner in which their characters echo the beliefs of the people of the time. In Paradise Lost, Satan is a supporter of the Puritan cause. As the Puritans did with Charles I, Satan attempts to over-throw what he believes to be a tyrant king. Another example is the way in which Satan refers to a belief that, in Milton's time, was "dear to men."[17] When Satan enters Hell for the first time, he cries:

> Hail horrors, hail
> Infernal world, and thou profoundest Hell
> Receive thy new Possessor; One who brings
> A mind not to be chang'd by Place or Time.
> The mind is its own place, and in itself
> Can make a Heav'n of Hell, a Hell of Heav'n.[18]

This was the popular belief of Milton's time—that it was the set of a person's own mind that determined whether he was happy or unhappy, not a place or time.[19]

Similarly, this technique appears again in Byron's works. All of Byron's heroes, no matter what evil they have done, stand as examples of the popular Romantic hero—a fiercely independent, rebellious individual who defies authority and who sets out on his own. In fact, the

Popham 6

Byronic hero is a reminder of Milton's Satan in that both are wanderers, loners, and outcasts of society. Satan, of course, is an outcast of Heaven. Even the title <u>Paradise Lost</u> seems to be a woeful reminder that man is not the only one who lost paradise.

Thorslev says that Byron's <u>Childe Harold</u> "has an echo" of <u>Paradise Lost</u>'s Satan.[20] <u>Childe Harold</u> is considered the "first important Byronic hero" and the "prototype for all the rest."[21] Of <u>Childe Harold I</u> and <u>II</u>, Thorslev further adds that the hero shows no "final consistency of character or outlook," but that in <u>Childe Harold III</u> and <u>IV</u>, he has "rejected order in preference of skepticism, reason, and freedom."[22] Childe Harold is the "wandering outlaw of his own darkmind."[23] The society in which he lives exiles him, so he in turn rejects it to live a life of "proud solitude."[24] Cain is an exile, too, turned away by his own people to be a reject of humanity.

Cain, of course, is rejected because of his sin, which is deemed by God to be unforgivable—the jealous murder of his brother. This is an example of another similarity between Milton's Satan and the Byronic hero—both are haunted by their past wrongs. The beauty of this is that neither Satan nor Byron's heroes will admit that they have committed a wrong. Perhaps this is because neither Milton nor Byron really feels they have. Satan attempts to overthrow God, and as a result, is condemned forever to exile in Hell. Certainly, his deed will haunt him forever simply because he can never return to paradise.

Popham 7

In a similar way, Cain will always be haunted by his deed because he must spend the rest of his life in exile from society. Both Satan and Cain, however, accept their punishment proudly, as though it were an honor to be rejected by a society that they so desperately despise. The bottom line is that neither Satan nor Cain is sorry.

Manfred is another Byronic hero who is haunted by a past deed. Like a "typical Byronic hero," he is "haunted by a remorse from some dark crime."[25] The storyline hints that he may have committed incest with his sister, an interesting change because Byron himself was accused of incest with his half-sister, Augusta Leigh.[26] Manfred searches for his sister who has run away, and when he finally finds her, he dies upon seeing her. Manfred possesses a soul tortured by his own deed, and yet he refuses to repent. He dies rejecting both the demons of Hell and the Christian religion.

This is an example of the way in which both Milton's Satan and Byron's heroes reject authority and the establishment. The Satan of Paradise Lost scorns the whole idea of regulated, ordered authority in which the ruler has no justified right to rule. He says that he "reigns" in Hell, but this seems to be only because he has earned the position by taking the lead in the rebellion. Where Byron's heroes are concerned, this still seems to hold true. The people in Byron's works "submit" to his heroes because "they recognize leadership, even in one who is for independence and individual freedom."[27]

Popham 8

Similarly, Anne Radcliffe, a Romantic novelist, displays her views of the establishment in <u>The Italian</u>. Her Romantic hero would rather live in his own tortured world than "accept a world where cause and effect are providentially and naturally ordered."[28] This Romantic interpretation is one that Byron shares. He blames the establishment and corrupt rulers for the sins of his heroes. "The typical political situation [or the Byronic work] is that the evils of despotism produce criminals or outlaws but that crime, through not condoned, is less wicked, less hypocritical, than the society which produces it."[29] Certainly, this holds true for Byron's <u>Cain</u>. The story seems to imply that Cain was "forced into murder by opposition to God" and that because "evil procures evil," God is really at fault for Cain's weaknesses, as is the society that worships him.[30] It is also true of Don Juan, a "hero who belongs to no social order" who would "castigate the British 'establishment' from a personal position of exile."[31] In <u>The Vision of Judgment</u>, Byron's hero cries, "God save the king!" The passages after that statement suggest that God had better save the king because the king is a sinner who needs saving. In <u>Childe Harold</u>, the Byronic hero claims, "I am as a weed, flung from a rock."[32] This seems to suggest that Harold is "a victim of circumstances rather than the master of his fate."[33] So, Milton seems to imply, is Satan.

As previously mentioned, Shelly says that his Prometheus most closely resembles Milton's Satan. Thorslev also says that Shelly's Prometheus is a Byronic hero because he is "an individual, skeptic, and rebel."[34] Milton's Satan is considered, especially in the Romantic Age, to be the hero of <u>Paradise Lost</u>. Many poets and writers have modeled their heroes on the idea of an independent, rebellious, wandering character who scorns authority and lives his life away from society. Byron's heroes go far beyond the classical model of a Romantic hero. Because of the era in which he lived, Milton was not able to air his views clearly on what a hero should be, or so Byron thought. During the rebellious Romantic Age, Milton's Satanic hero "came into style." In view of their similar attitudes, values, and actions, it is clear that Byron based his heroes, not just on a common Romantic theme, but on Milton's Satanic hero in particular, attempting to restate the beliefs that he felt Milton had said only vaguely in <u>Paradise Lost</u>.

Byron believed that "a poet's first moral duty is to the truth."[35] More than anything, Byron wanted to state the truth about life and society. He believed that Milton knew the truth, and he wanted everyone, through his works, to be sure of that truth.

Popham 10

Notes

[1]Peter L. Thorslev, Jr., <u>The Byronic Hero</u> (U.S.A.: Lund, 1962) 111.

[2]Thorslev 109.

[3]Thorslev 110.

[4]"Milton," <u>Encyclopedia Britannica</u>, 1988 ed.

[5]Thorslev 111.

[6]Julian Hill, <u>Great English Poets</u> (London: Richards, 1907) 233.

[7]"English Literature," <u>Encyclopedia Britannica</u>, 1988 ed.

[8]Thorslev 178.

[9]Thorslev 110.

[10]"English Literature," <u>Encyclopedia Britannica</u>, 1988 ed.

[11]John Milton, <u>Paradise Lost</u> (New York: Odyessey, 1935) 18.

[12]Malcolm Kelsall, "George Gordon, Lord Byron, <u>Cain</u>," <u>British Writers</u>, ed. Ian Scott-Kilbert, vol. 4 (New York: Scribner's, 1981) 181.

[13]Kelsall 181.

[14]Kelsall 181.

[15]Joseph Natoli, "William Blake," Critical Survey of Poetry, vol. 4. (Englewood Cliffs: Salem, 1982) 218.

[16]John M. Steadman, <u>Milton and the Paradoxes of Renaissance Heroism</u> (Baton Rouge: L.S.U.P, 1987) 113.

[17]Milton 17.

Popham 11

[18]Milton 17.

[19]Milton 17.

[20]Thorslev 131.

[21]Thorslev 128.

[22]Thorslev 122.

[23]Kelsall 175.

[24]Kelsall 176.

[25]Kelsall 179.

[26]"Byron" Encyclopedia Britannica, 1988 ed.

[27]Kelsall 175.

[28]E. B. Murray, Anne Radcliffe (New York: Twayne, 1982) 158.

[29]Murray 158.

[30]Kelsall 181.

[31]Kelsall 171.

[32]Kelsall 176.

[33]Kelsall 176.

[34]Thorslev 124.

[35]Kelsall 189.

Popham 12

Bibliography

"Byron." <u>Encyclopedia Britannica</u>. 1988 ed.

"English Literature." <u>Encyclopedia Britannica</u>. 1988 ed.

Hill, Julian. <u>Great English Poets</u>. London: E. Grant
      Richards, 1907.

Kelsall, Malcolm. "Gordon, George, Lord Byron, <u>Cain</u>."
      <u>British Writers</u>, ed. Ian Scott-Kilbert. Vol. 4. New
      York: Scribner's 1981.

"Milton." <u>Encyclopedia Britannica</u>. 1988 ed.

Milton, John. <u>Paradise Lost</u>. New York: Odyessey, 1935.

Murray, E. B. <u>Anne Radcliffe</u>. New York: Twayne, 1972.

Natoli, Joseph. "William Blake." <u>Critical Survey of
      Poetry</u>. Vol. 1. Englewood Cliffs: Salem, 1982.

Steadman, John M. <u>Milton and the Paradoxes of Renaissance
      Heroism</u>. Baton Rouge: L.S.U.P., 1987.

Thorslev, Peter J., Jr. <u>The Byronic Hero</u>. U.S.A.: Lund,
      1962.

Index